Winning Over Life's Challenges

DR. SANDRA L. BAILEY

authorHOUSE®

AuthorHouse™
1663 Liberty Drive
Bloomington, IN 47403
www.authorhouse.com
Phone: 1 (800) 839-8640

Published by AuthorHouse 07/29/2019

ISBN: 978-1-7283-2096-0 (sc)
ISBN: 978-1-7283-2094-6 (hc)
ISBN: 978-1-7283-2095-3 (e)

Library of Congress Control Number: 2019910677

Print information available on the last page.

CONTENTS

DEDICATION

To my daughter Sanian who I am so privileged to have mothered for the past twenty-two years. You have been an inspiration to me over the years, and unintentionally motivated and encouraged me to endure some of the winters that I had to go through. Unintentional motivation, because many times during my winter seasons you were at the forefront of my thoughts because I desperately wanted to get through it for you. My reason for surviving was not only to see you grow up. It was primarily for you to understand the importance of being resilient in the challenges that you will face in life.

San, life is not a bed of roses, the streets are not always paved with gold, and everything will not always go your way. The fact that God allows you to go through life's winter, it means that He can trust you with life. His word declares, *"Man that is born of a woman is of few days and full of trouble,"* (Job 14:1). Trouble is inescapable. This book will encourage you to recognize that you can WIN over life's challenges if you put God first. You must face your winter with the knowledge that winter does not change God's plan and objective for your life. It simply means that He is preparing you for the next dimension.

San, I love you and truly wish that I could protect you from all of life's winters. The reality is I am unable. However, I know God can! My prayer is that you will continue to commit the keeping of your life to Him, because He promised that He would provide you grace and warmth in your time of need. Do not fear the cold that comes with the winter. Equip yourself with the word of God and surround yourself with individuals of like precious faith. This is the winning formula to get through it! I believe you CAN, and I know you WILL!

Love you Sanian!
Your helicopter Mom!

ACKNOWLEDGEMENTS

The title of this book *"When Winter Comes - Wining Over Life's Challenges,"* came to me six years ago. After co-authoring two devotionals and being hesitant about sharing my challenges it is finally published. The journey was long, I have preached, talked and testified about it, whetting my hearers' appetites, leaving them asking when the book is coming out. Well, if you are reading this acknowledgement, it is finally here. Thanks, be unto God who ALWAYS causes me to triumph! His leading and constant reminder that I am blessed to be a blessing, allowed me to lay aside my personal preference of being private, to write this book. With God's help I was able to peel back the curtains of my life so that others can peer in and see what God can do for someone who trust Him.

Special mention, to my husband Ian, and my daughter Sanian for their understanding and love. You afforded me the freedom to write whenever I felt like it. Thanks for standing with me as I endured some of the winter seasons mentioned in this book. You were God's hands, eyes and ears for me during some of these struggles. Undoubtedly, I could not have survived some of these winters without you. I love you deeply and cannot imagine life without you both. Let us continue to stay together, so that we can provide warmth for each other.

Sher, God knew what He was doing when He allowed our paths to cross. This coming together has generated positive results, over the last five years. Your areas of strengths have complimented my areas of weakness. This allowed me to reach deep down on the inside to do things that I talked about and dreamed of for a long time. This book is a prime example and would not be completed without your labor of love. From being the captain of the cheer leading squad, editor, encourager, and unhesitatingly writing the foreword, I thank you! I love you and cherish the precious friendship that we share. Let us continue to prayerfully blaze trails together!

Stacy Buckley, thanks for being here for me from day one! You are an example of what it truly means to be a rock-solid friend. Thanks for sharing your fleece in some of my winter experiences. It kept me warm, so today I can share my story. Your constant reminder that I had a book to finish helped me to never lose sight of that fact. I love you and appreciate all that you do!

Shakera Sharpe and Nicholette Collins – Dryden, thanks for your additional pairs of eyes in reviewing and editing of this manuscript. Your attention to detail and quick turnaround time made a positive impact on the outcome of this book. I love and appreciate you both.

To everyone who has been there for me over the years, in whatever capacity. Your love, care, concern, encouragement, prayers and support served as warmth to help me endure and thrive in my many winters. I honestly would not have made it without the people in my village of which YOU are a part. Today, I can share my journey because of what you all did for me when I could not have done it for myself. You aided in my survival. I love you all and please know that I am forever grateful!

Thanks to all those who will read this book, your investment will not be a waste. My prayer is that within the pages of this book you will find words of encouragement, and practical tips to help you get through your winter season. Stay warm!

FOREWORD

I have heard it said that nobody trips over a mountain; it is the pebbles along the way that cause you to stumble. Pass all the pebbles in your path and you will conquer your mountain. "When Winter Comes," will help you learn how to pass the pebbles. Dr. Sandra Bailey's life experiences have made her a virtuoso in understanding how to navigate the seasons of life. With a freeing transparency, Sandra shares stories from her life that will resonate with you. She writes in such a way that you will feel the cold air hit you as she disembarks the plane in Boston, Massachusetts for the first time. Do not be surprised if hot tears roll down your cheeks when you read her account of going through a financial winter.

If you have read any of her previous books, ("Called to Worship ~ A Lifestyle of Praise," "Overcoming Job Loss ~ A Spiritual Guide," "Water's Edge Volume I and II ~ A 31 Day Devotional), you will know that faith, family and friends are essential to her winterizing process. She does not leave the reader with the false notion that winter will be a walk in the park. Instead, she honestly shares from her experiences, exposing us to the harsh realities of what we may encounter when going through our winter seasons. Sandra blankets us with encouragement, warms the heart with faith-filled anecdotes, and reminds us that winter will not last forever.

"When Winter Comes ~ Overcoming Life's Challenges," is like a steaming cup of hot chocolate with mini-marshmallows on a cold, dark night. It calms the mind and will put a sweet smile on your soul. Go ahead take a sip and read from cover to cover. You will not be disappointed.

Enjoying my cup,

Water's Edge Network, LLC

INTRODUCTION

In 1990 I migrated from the beautiful island of Jamaica which is surrounded by the Caribbean Sea where it is consistently warm tropical weather. This appealing weather along with the laid-back culture make Jamaica a popular tourist destination. With the harshness of the winter season in some countries, we see an increase in tourist presence as they relax and let their hair down. While vacationing, they would lay out on our nice white sandy beaches and soak up hours of sun as they relax to some reggae music and island cuisine. The nice island breeze, along with the friendliness of the natives makes Jamaica a place to escape the hustle and bustle of everyday life. I loved living in Jamaica! This was the only home I knew, where the popular phrase was, "Jamaica NO problem."

My mother and one of my older brother and sister were already living in the United States of America. They all worked hard and pooled their financial resources together to aid in the migration of myself and my other siblings. Leading up to my migration to join them I had numerous coaching sessions from "experienced" individuals who have had the opportunity to travel to the United States during the winter season. The lecture was about how cold it can be during the winter months and how prepared I should be. Even my inexperienced natives were extending their warnings about the cold weather. I remember landing at the airport in May. After clearing immigration, I made my way through the large rotating doors to the outside where my ride was waiting for me. As I stepped outside, the cold wind greeted me angrily and almost blew me away literally! At that time, I only weighed about ninety-nine pounds. I grabbed on to the nearest pole, as I tried to regain my composure. Everyone around me seemed to be unbothered by the wind as they went about their business. After the initial hugging, greeting and the exuberant welcome to America we headed home. Throughout all this I was feeling cold and missing my friends back home.

The next morning, I woke up to bright sunshine and very clear skies, a memory of home in Jamaica. With that kind of view from the window I was eager to go on the outside to explore my new environment. This was now going to be home for me. I hurriedly had something to eat and my sister Jackie who was already residing here for many years decided to take us for a walk to the town square. I was totally deceived by the sunshine as I stepped outside, it was cold, and I was freezing as I was dressed in summer attire. My sister went back in the house and got us jackets, they were heavy and oversized, but they kept us warm.

The weeks ahead I wore winter clothing and dressed in layers, but nothing prepared me for this kind of cold. I would complain to everyone that came by to meet us how cold it was, to which they all responded that it was not cold, instead it was "nice out." Immediately, my response would be, "if this is not cold I do not want to experience winter." As spring came around it became warmer. I began to feel a little more at home and by summer I felt like I was at home for real. Enjoying the barbeques, the meet and greet, going shopping and visiting other family members created an escape as I lost myself in the warmness of summer. This reminded me so much of my exotic homeland, Jamaica. The cold I felt that night in May was shelved in the back of my mind and I was enjoying the current season. When fall rolled around with the help of coats, tights, dressing in layers of clothing and boots I was able to tolerate the cold, but it became tough for me when winter came.

When winter came I took out my winter boots, gloves, winter hats, scarfs, sweaters, ear muffs and anything that would keep me warm and wore them. I was prepared, but I was still shaking from the cold. I never knew it could have gotten as cold as it did. The sight of snow for the first time was not fascinating or intriguing. Appreciating the beauty of the snow paled in comparison to me seeking to be warm and wishing for my eighty – ninety degree weather. My first couple of winters were harsh and challenging; I would dread it especially when I had to walk in the snow coupled with gusty winds and freezing rain. During the winter months I would be mad at myself for migrating to the United States, because after all I had a great life in Jamaica without all this cold and snow. I scoffed at the phrase that I was here to have a "better life." How could this be a better life I thought, when we had to gingerly navigate our way on ice, having near misses with slips and falls, and having my contact lenses falling out in the snow from being too dry. Not to mention having to drive in the snow and holding on for dear life. Seriously feeling homesick, I often found myself sad and regretful.

Twenty-eight years later living in this country, I have adopted the seasonal cycles and adjusted my mind set. As I enjoy the seasons of spring, summer and fall I do so very well knowing that winter is sure to come sometime in December. It was not a matter if winter comes but, I was preparing for WHEN winter comes. My preparation for the natural winter did not remove the cold and harshness of the season, all it did was helped me to go through it with more knowledge and a better attitude. Very few individuals look forward to the winter season. Cold, inclement weather combined with increased sickness and long dark days can induce loneliness and depression. Previously green grass and plants all morph to ugly, drab colors, taking our cheerful outlook with them. We long for sunshine and spring, flowers and warmth, but winter seems unending. Yet the Bible says that, *"While the earth remaineth, seedtime and harvest, and cold and heat, and summer and winter, and day and night shall not cease,"* (Genesis 8:22).

My personal surrender and walk with the Lord spans over thirty-seven years. The very first time someone told me that the situation I was going through was "just a season," I was convinced they had no clue. I was young in my faith and could not relate. Honestly, I felt like that was just a way to brush me off or make light of what I was going through. How could what I was feeling be just a season? Little did I know that synonymous to winter in the natural, one would encounter winter in the spiritual. I was genuinely hurting and felt like everything that could go wrong was going wrong. During that time, I found myself questioning not only my faith but also if God really cared. In surrendering my life to God, I thought that would only yield moments of peace and happiness because I was void of the scripture that states, *"Yea, and all that will live godly in Christ Jesus shall suffer persecution," (*2 Timothy 3:12).

The more I sought after God and grew in spiritual maturity, I came to realize that the individual was right, it was just a season. With the knowledge that I have gleaned through reading, hearing the preached word, testimonies of fellow believers and studying the word of God, came clarity. I understood that the seasons of nature are often reflected in the seasons of our lives as believers. All the spiritual giants I have encountered personally or by reading about them, have had periods in their spiritual lives during which they felt very distant in their relationship with God. These are often called drought spells, wilderness experience or desert times, which can be accompanied by feelings of abandonment, despair, and discouragement. We are no different than these great men and women of God for in much the same way, you and I will go through spiritually dormant seasons. During these seasons it appears like God is silent. It appears dark and cold, and at times it leaves us shivering and longing for warmer days. It is then we realize that our winter has come.

Winter is one of the four seasons of the year. It is the coldest season in the northern hemisphere from December to February and in the southern hemisphere from June to August, and it occurs before spring and after fall. It may be one of the least liked or most feared seasons by individuals. During this season the vibrant colors have ebbed away leaving only colors like brown, white, grey and black. Winter can also can be a lonely time for many people because there might be less interaction with others daily. People go straight home from work and huddle in for the night to escape the elements that come along with winter.

Studies show that nearly one in ten people who suffer from Seasonal Affective Disorder – SAD (or from winter depression), their malaise stems more from this lack of light than it does from the cold. It is hard on all of us to go from fourteen-hour days to days with nine hours or less of sunlight. Regardless of these challenges, winter has much to offer for those who work in agriculture. Although this weather appears to be an inconvenience and unpleasant it is very necessary for farmers and their crops. They know that a warm winter means that the soil's moisture will not be recharged, the larvae of insects will not be killed and so the cycle of their whole planting season will be altered. Things planted in the fall also need that time of dormancy to allow them to grow healthier and more robust in the spring. The Bible states, *"Unless a grain of wheat fall into the ground and die, it abideth alone; but if it die, it bringeth forth much fruit."* (St John 12:24). Your winter will determine the success of your harvest.

As harsh and uninviting as winter may seem unless we go through the winter we cannot have spring. Although we may not see or feel anything exciting during this dormant season, it does not mean that nothing is happening. It simple means winter has come. We should approach this season with the understanding that it can teach us lessons on strength, endurance, growth, faith, and trust. See it as a time of preparation, patience, renewal and as an ordained season of your life and not an act of punishment from God. If we can view winter through those lenses, it will help you to cope and enjoy the blessings that the season brings.

As harsh and uninviting as winter may seem unless we go through the winter we cannot have spring.

It is during our winter season that our inner character is developed and strengthened. Winter allows us to lay aside the capes and be vulnerable and transparent before our God. A strong Christlike character is essential for withstanding storms that will come during seasons of growth. After the winter, we are going to need the strength to carry out the harvest.

We do run the risk of dying during the harvest if we did not strengthen ourselves during the winter. I find there are a lot of people who have the gifts and talents to take them somewhere exciting, but if they do not have strong Christian principles all the talent in the world will not sustain them in that space of prominence.

Everyone experiences difficulties, setbacks, and moments of hardship in their lives, and this can put a strain on a person's relationship with God and those around them. Christians experiencing hardship may find it easier to put their religion on the backburner while they work through their problems, but this is not what God wants us to do. Feeling isolated is one of the toughest parts of the winter season. It can feel like you are all alone in your pain, and that makes it so much worse. The comfort of those who have known that same pain is inexpressible, their reassuring words feels like a warm blanket being draped around your soul. For someone to say those powerful words like, "I know just how you feel because I have been there," that person had to endure the same difficult winter season.

That winter you are currently facing, whether it is struggles in your marriage, friendships, relationships, finances, career or with your health is bearable. You can endure and overcome. The question is, how do we navigate this season? The cold winds of winter were never designed to blow you out of the presence of God but rather to blow you in His arms where you can find warmth to sustain you.

> ***The cold winds of winter were never designed to blow you out of the presence of God but rather to blow you in His arms where you can find warmth to sustain you.***

He never promised us a winter – free life but He promised to be with us to the very end. The word of God assures us that He will never leave us or forsake us. So, wrap yourself in the blanket of His love and remember, God is that burning bush even on the coldest of winter days. He became a pillar of fire by night to provide light and warmth during the night for the children of Israel, (Exodus 13:21-22). Call to remembrance that the same God who blesses us in the spring, summer and fall is the same God who will bless us in the winter; He never changes. Your hardship does not mean God has forgotten you. It means He has a future for you, and you will need the experience of winter to aid you as you move towards your destiny.

Wrap yourself in the blanket of His love and remember, God is that burning bush even on the coldest of winter days.

My hope is that from the pages of this book some warmth will come your way. I am sharing my own fleece with you to provide you some added support as you go through your winter seasons. At times we see the harvest of others, but we do not know the winter that they had to endure to get to that bountiful return. Occasionally, God must let you experience winter to accelerate your harvest. Winter was never meant to freeze your hope, destroy your dreams or abort your destiny. Instead it is meant to strengthen your roots. With your roots being strengthened when the winds and storms come, you will be able to stand firm.

Stop looking over the fence at your neighbors' spring and summer seasons and wondering why you must go through winter. Consider it a part of the process towards your destiny. The truth is some winters are harsher than others but know that no one escapes winter, it is a must. As you read through the pages of

The truth is some winters are harsher than others but know that no one escapes winter, it is a must.

this book my prayer is that you will find warmth, hope and assurance that **WHEN** your winter comes you will go through it without fear but with the grace called confidence. Winter will not last forever because spring is coming. Through my own personal and transparent experiences, I pray that you will be encouraged to enjoy and embrace the beauty and benefits of the winter and refrain from rushing the season.

CHAPTER ONE

"Beloved, I wish above all things that thou mayest prosper and be in health, even as thy soul prospereth." 3 John 2

I have often heard the phrase, "if you do not have good health you have nothing," however prior to being saved I would have believed this statement wholeheartedly. After coming to know Christ and trusting Him to be the God of all flesh who nothing is too hard for. I now view that statement through a new set of lenses. I do believe that good health is important because a lot of our survival and life depends on it. The Bible states in 3 John 2, *"Beloved, I wish above all things that thou mayest prosper and be in health, even as thy soul prospereth."* God wants us to enjoy the blessings of good health. He is not only concerned with our spiritual lives, but He takes care of us wholistically and even knows the number of hairs on our head.

After encountering a few health scares of my own and have watched loved ones struggle through the winter of their health, I view the statement, *"if you do not have good health you have nothing"* with hope, because God is our everything. The statement is no longer absolute for me as a believer. No one is hopeless whose hope is in God. Knowing that God is the Great Physician, the Balm in Gilead, the sympathizing Jesus and He can be touched by the feelings of our infirmities, changes my perspective on how I manage through these times. Accepting the Lord at the age of seventeen afforded me the opportunity to witness the healing power of God in the lives of many believers. At times I sat in awe of some of the big wins for my God. Having the opportunity to see the cripple walk, the blind eyes see and the deaf hear. This was not just something I read in the Bible but that which I witnessed.

During my childhood, I remember being sick and having to be admitted in the hospital for several weeks. I hated the experience and would be so afraid at nights when my mother left for home. I thought I was going to die during the night. At that age I was not saved, and I had no understanding of hell and heaven I just knew that I did not want to be in the hospital and I did not want to die. One night a young girl died next to me and the following night I was so scared I thought that I would be next. Upon my mother's arrival that evening, I cried and begged her to take me home. Shortly after, the doctor came and made his rounds and decided that I was well enough to go home. I was very happy to be back home in my familiar surroundings. I had no relationship with God but inwardly I prayed that I would never experience that kind of sickness again.

Moving forward, for most of my life I rarely experienced any worry surrounding my health. My body did what it was supposed to do. Being a child of God I made healthy life choices, like refraining from smoking and drinking. Ensuring that I took care of my body knowing it is the temple of the living God. I rarely got sick and I exercised occasionally. The fact that health problems were never even on my radar, when problems started to arise in my health I felt like winter had come. The arrival of winter in my health spun me a confusing cycle of anxiety, uncertainty, and worry. I remember going for my routine mammography exam, something I dreaded doing because of the pain that was associated with it. I went to have it done on a Wednesday and usually I would receive the results in the mail within one week.

It was the Friday of the same week I was on my way home from work and I stopped at the Chinese Buffet to get some shrimp and crab legs, my favorite. My intention was to go home eat and unwind after a long work week. Upon my arrival home, there was the day's mail on the kitchen counter and as always, I sieved through to take mine. Within the pile was a letter from the hospital Breast Center, I gingerly opened the mail and began reading. As I read the tears began flowing down my cheek as the content was not the usual see you next year. Instead it stated that I had to come back for further testing as soon as possible. I was numb, worn out, and feeling like every ounce of life had been sucked out of me. The crab legs and shrimp that initially I so eagerly wanted to devour meant nothing anymore. I remember curling up in bed with the letter and kept reading it over and over thinking that the words would change magically. I silently cried myself to sleep fearing the unknown.

It was the longest weekend I ever had and on Monday morning I made the appointment. The first available date was a week out to which I begged and pleaded to see if I could get an earlier date but to no avail. At church the following Sunday I asked two Missionaries who I confided in to intercede on my behalf. Being very transparent with them I shared what was going on and how fearful I was. I knew that God was a healer and He can do all things but now that I was the one facing winter in my health I began to struggle. It became so difficult for me to remain in a posture of complete trust. The day of my follow up testing I went alone because I did not want to alarm anyone, my five to seven minutes ride felt like an eternity as a mirage of thoughts and what ifs were racing through my mind. At one point I had to verbally encourage myself by saying, "I know whatever befalls me Jesus doeth all things well." This helped me somewhat to put my mind at ease.

Upon entering the facility, the staff was very friendly and chirpy for a Monday morning as they instructed me on what to do. I went through a series of testing and had to wait for a while. Anxiety and fear engulfed me, and I found myself crying as I was imagining the worst news mingled with hope that everything was going to be fine. I was called in for my consultation with the doctor who told me that the tests/biopsy they performed was inconclusive and I had to have a surgical biopsy done. Trying to fight back tears I asked the doctor a few questions, thanked her and left the office. When I got to my car with tears falling from my eyes, I surrendered everything to God. I felt myself breathlessly running after God. Every fiber of my being wanted to pursue Him. I invited God into every part of me, into every crevice and every piece I had been trying to keep under my control. I needed Him more than ever and I believed that He was the only one that was going to see me through these winter months.

That evening I sat with my husband and explained to him what was going on with me. With his strong unwavering faith in God, He looked at me and held me saying, "You are going to be alright, do not worry." A part of me wanted to believe him and fear on the other hand prevented me from doing so. I was about to open my mouth and express that fear to him when the Holy Spirit reminded me that death and life is in the power of the tongue, (Proverb 18:21) and that our lives are framed by our words. In the days ahead, I began to research doctors who conducted this kind of surgery and their expertise, how long they have been practicing and just general reviews about them. I finally settled on one that was the head of oncology at the hospital I was planning to have the surgery done.

Eagerly wanting this ordeal to be behind me, I called to make an appointment and he was able to consult with me in a couple of days. Again, I acted brave and went to the consultation alone. As I walked in his office, I lost it and just started crying. I handed him the films and results from the previous testing and he began asking me a few questions. Submerged by my emotions and fears I became choked up when answering the questions. He got up from his desk and came over and laid his hand on my shoulder assuring me that I was going to be fine. He told me he could perform the surgery, but he would not be able to tell me anything definitive until after the surgery and the biopsy was done. I could not believe what I was hearing, I wanted answers and comfort. He walked me over to his assistant, so I could get the first available date he had to perform the surgery. The first appointment was one month out, immediately I started crying to the secretary and telling her that I could not wait that long. She told me she understood but that is the best she could do because he was booked solid. Hope came through when she told me if someone canceled I would be next in line.

On the drive home, I began talking with God, I was very open and transparent with Him, I told Him that I no longer wanted fear and stress to be in the driver's seat on this journey. I asked Him to increase my faith so that I can totally trust Him, I confessed according to Psalm 31:15 that my times were in His hands. In that moment I chose to say no to the lies and to the fears that the enemy was trying to bring upon me. I chose to say no to myself as I kept trying to take over and be in control of what was not my burden to bear, God said that we should cast all our cares upon Him because He careth for us (1 Peter 5:7). I was determined in that moment that I had two choices either continue down this dark path I had allowed myself to enter, or I could turn around and run towards God. As difficult as it was I chose to give it all to God.

The following day my phone rang, and it was the doctor's secretary on the other end of the line. She had good news for me, someone had cancelled, and I could have my surgery a week from that day if I was able to get all my pre-op work done. Silently, I thanked God for answered prayers. I got everything completed in a timely manner and was ready for my surgery the following Tuesday. The day of the surgery my husband and I arrived at the hospital on time. He stayed with me chatting and giving me jokes until it was time for me to go in the operating room. As I was being wheeled in I became very emotional as involuntary tears rolled down my cheek, my husband kissed me and declared that I would be fine. In the operating room the doctor along with his staff attempted to put me at ease. The anesthesiologist asked me what I was having done. I responded and the next thing I knew I woke up in the recovery room. I was in pain with a terrible sore throat and extremely thirsty.

Disoriented and asking where I was the nurse came over and explained to me that the surgery was over, and I was in recovery. She said that my husband would be able to see me in the next half an hour, I told her I was in pain and she gave me some pain medicine. Falling in and out of sleep for another hour I finally became fully awake and my husband was now at my bedside. The doctor came in to say that the surgery was successfully, but they had to wait on pathology results which could take up to a week. Hearing that I was crushed because I wanted the answers NOW! so I can move on with my life. I felt like my life had been on hold for the last month and a half. I desperately wanted this winter season to be over and done. Why did I have to go through this? What have I done to deserve this? These were just a few of the questions that plagued me.

The days between the surgery and obtaining the results felt like eternity. I felt isolated, sad and fearful. When I was around individuals I acted like everything was fine but, on the inside, I was sad, frightened and overwhelmed. I never left my phone out of my sight because I did not want to miss that call from the doctor's office. I consistently prayed and asked God to make the results be favorable. I knew that God's plan is perfect, and he has no obligation to update me with the details. However, there was still some degree of fear of the unknown looming over me. Each time fear presented itself I would encourage myself with the word of God. I had gone through the Bible and extracted and memorized scriptures that spoke to the healing power and promises of God.

Those scriptures brought me comfort and got me through the waiting period, they literally kept me warm in those dark and cold winter nights. They represented hope for me. The Friday evening about 6:00 pm the phone rang, and it was the doctor's office. The call that I was waiting on was finally coming through and here I was frozen and afraid to take it. On what seemed to be the final ring I answered, the familiar voice of the secretary said, "Your results came in." I was speechless! She asked if I was still there I said, "Yes," she said, "EVERYTHING came back negative." I gave out a loud, "Thank you Jesus!" She said, "I know how the wait feels for these things that is why I wanted to catch you before we go into the weekend." She ended by saying that I needed to schedule a breast ultrasound every six months just to ensure nothing had changed.

Kneeling by my bedside that evening after hanging up the phone I thanked God for His mercies and His love towards me. Amid thanking Him I asked Him to forgive me for not trusting Him totally when I was going through the process. Humbly, I begged Him for grace to trust Him more. This experience was a time of growth for me as I was forced to trust God even when it seemed like I could not trace Him. After this documented experience, I have had another instance of winter in my health where I had to have surgery, but I went through that with so much more grace based on my experience. This did not mean that I did not have days when I was down or even had a few questions for God. I have always known that my fertility was a gift from God because I have known individuals who were unable to conceive so when I had my daughter I counted it a great blessing. We have been blessed to never struggle with infertility and we gave God thanks for His blessings. In my late forties I began to have very painful menstrual cycles and the blood flow would be so extremely heavy. However, I never took it as an indication that something was wrong.

As this got progressively worst month after month I remember making an appointment with my gynecologist to discuss my symptoms. He ordered me to have a vaginal ultra sound and once the results were in he would review them. The day of the ultra sound the technician took what I thought was forever to complete the ultrasound. This prompted me to ask her if everything was okay. She was very polite and told me that my doctor would discuss the results with me. I understood the medical protocol that she was not a doctor and that sharing the results was outside of her job description.

A cafeteria of thoughts flooded my mind, what was she seeing that she could not share with me. I spent the days between the ultra sound and the doctor's visit, one week to be exact, wondering what was causing the pain and heavy bleeding. Again, I employed my faith to work for me. Honestly, there were days when I lapsed into self-pity, self-doubt, and worst-case scenarios as I endured the wait.

The results came in and that day I entered the doctor's office with my self-diagnoses that I had fibroids. However, I thought that was no big deal because I have heard of women having fibroids and continued to lead a normal life except for painful, heavy bleeding during menstruation. He went over my ultrasound results only to state the thing I had feared the most. For the pain and heavy bleeding to stop I had to have a hysterectomy. I was shocked! Although in theory I knew what a hysterectomy entailed, I still asked him for a detailed explanation. As he went through his explanation and the different ways this procedure could be done, tears began welling up in my eyes. I was now facing the reality of never again being able to carry a child even if I changed my mind. This was emotionally devasting and painful. You kind of need a uterus to do so, and mine he was saying had to be removed. He told me to think about it and I could have the surgery done within a month. I left the office very upset, hurt and a feeling like God had let me down and why me? My husband Ian and I were not planning on having any more children, but I still wanted my uterus. I felt like that defined me as a woman.

For months I was in denial and my painful monthly cycles were constant reminders of what was going on in my body. Ian was very supportive and was open to any decision I made. To do or not to do the surgery was my choice. I had confided in a few of my close friends and they also felt that I should do what was most comfortable for me. Coming to terms with this was so difficult and upsetting for me in so many ways. One evening when I was all alone I felt the worst pain ever, this pain had me doubled over in the bed, and at times kneeling on the floor. I tried just about anything that would bring me some relief. I cried out to God for His help as I faced this wintery time in my health, it was then that I decided that I was going to follow through with the surgery.

I had peace on most days about my upcoming surgery and as the date neared, I got more nervous. It was ironic that I felt the most sadness as I had my last period. The harsh reality seemed like it took the life out of me, I felt like I was being robbed of my womanhood. Why would I ever miss a period? Strange enough I did. However, I held on to the joy I have in the Lord knowing that He was working all things together for my good (Romans 8:28). I kept encouraging myself that my uterus did not define me and that I was still fearfully and wonderfully made. The night before the surgery I could not sleep. I said a prayer surrendering my uterus to God, I asked Him to help me to find peace and contentment with my decision. The Holy Spirit prompted me to give thanks because the Lord has blessed us with our beautiful daughter and there are still those who have never known the joy of bearing a child. The morning of the surgery I was filled with trepidation and anxiety as my husband attempted to reassure me that all would be well. I woke up in recovery after a successful surgery. I was in pain but was happy that there were no complications.

After all my vitals were stabilized, I was discharged that same evening. Physically, the road to recovery was great but to date I still struggle with the emotional pain. Taking comfort in the word of God has been my solace, source of strength, my joy and my peace. Today I sit in the truth of God's word. When the Lord Jesus Christ was facing the cross, His winter, He made out His last will and testament. Did you know He mentioned you in His will? He left you His peace: *"Peace I leave with you, my peace I give unto you: not as the world giveth, give I unto you. Let not your heart be troubled, neither let it be afraid,"* (John 14:27). His peace is supernatural, it is the peace that passes all understanding, and some days this peace shocks me. On days when my emotions became unraveled and out of sync, I draw on the heat of His peace like a thermal blanket to protect me from the chills of the winter.

A perfect example of how one should go through the winter season in your health is seen in the life of Job. Satan unleashed his attack on Job's health. We know that this disease changed Job's physical appearance because his friends were not able to recognize him, (Job 2:12). Not a single part of Job's body was unaffected by this disease. The text says that he was infected from the soles of his feet to the crown of his head. Not a single part of him could find rest from this disease, (Job 3:26; 30:17). Job then took a piece of broken pottery to scrape away the epidermal remnants of the diseased and infected skin. He also used it to scratch his skin that itched continually. This was a very harsh season in Job's health. Can you imagine having to deal with this day and night? Job's disease was compounded by his wife entering the picture and doing a little work for Satan. Instead of offering comfort to her husband as a good wife would do, she questioned whether he ought to remain faithful to his belief and suggest that he simply, "curse God and die" an alternative to enduring through such grief. This, of course, was exactly what Satan wanted Job to do. (Job 1:11).

In our winter season the devil wants us to curse God, He wants us to believe a lie, that God has failed us. Job knew the God that he served, and he had an answer for his wife. He knew that God was faithful, and he had a hope that he boldly declared in Job 19:26, *"And though after my skin worms destroy this body, yet in my flesh shall I see God."* As painful and as frustrating his declining health was He maintained his integrity and his faith in God. He knew that man that is born of a woman is of a few days and full of trouble. He also believed that the Lord giveth and the Lord taketh away and whichever way the pendulum swung, the name of the Lord should still be praised. We should never allow our winter to hide the blessings and the promises of God. Our confidence should remain secure and steadfast. He did not succumb to the strong winds of winter and the slippery ice but *"in all this Job sinned not, nor charged God foolishly."* (Job 1:22).

Job received a double portion blessing from the Lord for enduring His winter season. Job's path to the double portion was certainly a hard one. It had cost him many tears, heartaches, rejections, false accusations and struggles but in the end, it was worth it. Job's end was more blessed than his beginning, friendships, fortunes, family, and his future was restored. The life of Job teaches us that, although we cannot always understand the reason for our winters, we do have a God who can be trusted, who is Lord overall and who works all things for our good to bring us to that future day of glory and vindication.

All our winters may not end on the same high note as Job and the woman with the issue of blood, who only touched the hem of His garment, but nevertheless we will make it through. We may not get fifteen years like Hezekiah, our blind eyes may not be opened like Bartimaeus or our hearing may not be restored, but that does not mean that God has failed. Like Paul, He may give us His grace which is sufficient to keep us. Do not look for God to bring you through each winter season the same way. Remember His ways are not our ways, neither are His thoughts our thoughts, (Isaiah 55: 8-9). Take comfort in knowing that He will bring us out someway and somehow. The length of each winter season may be different but know that HE will provide you with wool to help you make it through to spring.

The length of each winter season may be different but know that HE will provide you with wool to help you make it through to spring.

Your first winter does prepare you for the others to come. My faith and confidence were strengthened from those difficulties which helped me to face the cold with bravery. If you are facing a winter season in your health, rather than giving your energy towards wishing for another season, trust God that He will bring you through safely. The surrender, although painful, positions us to receive all that God intends for that season much better than if we fight against it. God is always oriented towards our growth, even in our winter. The harshness of the season sometimes serves to strip away some of the things in our lives that are preventing us from going to the next dimension. Embrace your winter season. I guarantee you, a brighter day is coming where you will be able to enjoy and smell the roses of spring.

Focus Scriptures

"For God hath not given us the spirit of fear; but of power, and of love, and of a sound mind." **(2 Timothy 1:7).**

"And said, If thou wilt diligently hearken to the voice of the LORD thy God, and wilt do that which is right in his sight, and wilt give ear to his commandments, and keep all his statutes, I will put none of these diseases upon thee, which I have brought upon the Egyptians: for I am the LORD that healeth thee." **(Exodus 15:26).**

But he was wounded for our transgressions, he was bruised for our iniquities: the chastisement of our peace was upon him; and with his stripes we are healed. **(Isaiah 53:5).**

"Heal me, O Lord, and I shall be healed; save me, and I shall be saved: for thou art my praise." **(Jeremiah 17:14).**

"Confess your faults one to another, and pray one for another, that ye may be healed. The effectual fervent prayer of a righteous man availeth much." **(James 5:16).**

"And Jesus said unto him, Go thy way; thy faith hath made thee whole. And immediately he received his sight, and followed Jesus in the way." **(St. Mark 10:52).**

"Is any sick among you? Let him call for the elders of the church; and let them pray over him, anointing him with oil in the name of the Lord: And the prayer of faith shall save the sick, and the Lord shall raise him up; and if he have committed sins, they shall be forgiven him." **(James 5:14 – 15).**

CHAPTER TWO

Three weeks after arriving in the United States of America to Boston, Massachusetts I came to New Jersey for what I thought would be a visit with a church family I worshipped with in Jamaica. They had migrated to the States over ten years and were attending one of the branch churches of the church I attended in Jamaica. I was so filled with anticipation to see them and even more excited to be able to worship with them. On the day they were coming to pick me up in Boston, I packed my bag early and waited eagerly for their arrival. When the car pulled up, out came a man who introduced himself as the pastor of the church along with the wife of the family I knew. After greeting my mom and siblings that were at home that day, I kissed my mom goodbye and promised her I would call and see her soon.

Here I was, going to a place for the first time having no family members present just the church family I knew and now the pastor. Throughout the three and a half hours ride we conversed about the brethren I left in Jamaica and how they were doing. I also asked questions as I drove along the highway enjoying the beautiful scenery. Along the way, we stopped for food at a Rest Stop and to refresh ourselves. Upon re-entering the car a cafeteria of thoughts began to overwhelm me. I suddenly realized that I did not give my mom and siblings a definite time when I would be back home, and I only had fifty dollars to my name. Arriving at my destination, I took my meager belongings out of the car and bade farewell to the pastor.

Settling in was easy as I was showed to my room. I did not unpack my bag but decided to live out the bag for the week or two that I was planning to be there. I took a long hot shower, spoke to the family and then retired to my room. In my prayer that night I was very transparent with God. I asked Him to order my steps and not to open any door that He did not want me to walk through. I confessed to Him that I was missing home in Jamaica and did not want to live in America. Starting all over again was rough for me. I tossed and turned for most of the night. The thought that occupied my mind was what am I going to do with my life in this strange country. The enemy was desperately trying to bring fear upon me; however, I found comfort and assurance in the word of God, *"The eyes of the Lord are upon the righteous, and his ears are open unto their cry,"* (Psalm 34:15). With that thought resonating with me, I drifted off to sleep.

The next morning, we all got dressed and headed from New York to New Jersey where the couple worshipped to attend service. I really did not know what to expect even though I was told that it was a small church that was still in its formative phase. For me the ride was very long but the other passengers thought differently, when I made mention of the distance they had to travel. I felt it was because they were accustomed to it. When we got to the church, it was a huge and I felt good, only to find out that we were worshipping in the basement. Although this was a small assembly in comparison to where I was coming from, I immediately shifted my focus from the size of the congregation to giving God the worship and praise He deserved. I was introduced to the accepting congregants by the pastor and was asked to give greetings. I said I was happy to meet my brethren on this side of the vineyard and that I was here for a few weeks.

After being in New Jersey for two weeks and gotten acclimated to worshipping with the saints, it began to feel like home. I made a mental decision to stay in New Jersey because of the church and the fellowship, I love the Lord and I love the saints. I felt like the Lord wanted me to stay in New Jersey, however the hardest part of this was to communicate it to my mom and siblings back in Boston. Keep in mind I only knew the couple and another church brother from Jamaica. I remember praying that God would let my mom accept my decision to relocate in good faith. To no surprise of mine she hit the roof. She thought I had lost my mind and that I was making a terrible mistake because in her words, "How are you going to survive, you do not have a job, come home." I did go home but it was to get the remainder of my clothes. I was sure that this was what the Lord wanted me to do. My decision to relocate to New Jersey was a move of faith, like Abraham I was moving away from my family and everything I knew. (Genesis12:1). That day my mom was so hurt and disappointed, but more than anything she was worried that I did not have what it took financially to take care of myself. Of a truth she was perfectly right! I did not have a job and now only had $20.00 to my name.

I was worried too but I kept saying to myself, *"I was young and now I am old, and I have never seen the righteous forsaken nor His seed begging bread,"* (Psalm 37:25). I found every scripture I could think of that spoke to God's sustenance and recounted them. Being firm in my decision to live in New Jersey, upon my return I started seeking employment. I left the couple in New York and relocated to New Jersey. Stepping out on faith I rented a room from one of the church mothers with no job. Not knowing where I was going to get the funds to pay her, I told God that if He wanted me to stay here He would have to find a way to sustain me financially. In Jamaica I had a great job working in the telecommunication industry and here I was jobless and away from my biological family.

A month had passed since my relocation and I still did not have a job hence no income. Winter had come in my finances. Everything was bare and fruitless. Someone was nice enough to bless me with some funds to pay my rent and purchase food. Disappointed and sad that God would allow me to make this move and now here I was without money living out what my mom had said, depending on others. I was tempted to pack my meagre belongings and go back to Boston. My rationale was if I am going to depend on anyone it should be my family. Tears, fasting and prayer became my daily food. I was desperately trying to believe God. I was also engaged to be married in less than five months, so you know I needed the money. The more I applied for jobs the more I got rejection notices. Then one day finally I got a call for a per diem role at the local hospital as a Dietary Aide. Feeling subjugated to a role I was over credentialed for because I had a degree in Nutrition and Dietetics. I decided to accept it as I saw this as a way out. I needed the money.

Money answers all things, so I took all the hours I was offered to be able to pay my bills and save for my upcoming wedding. The struggle was real, I had to deny myself of what I considered some of the necessities of life. After all, I was now living in the United States, I never thought a day like this would come. This was supposed to be a country of plenty. I was living basically from paycheck to paycheck, but I held on to what God said, *"For I know the thoughts that I think toward you, says the Lord, thoughts of peace and not of evil, to give you a future and a hope,"* (Jeremiah 29:11). I employed my faith to work for me as I continued to work with my own hands, and at the same time trying to live the scripture, *"Godliness with contentment is great gain,"* (1 Timothy 6:6). God provided enough for me that I never had to call home for a loan, neither did I borrow from those around me. My handful of meal was able to sustain me until my harvest came.

Seven months later being in the United States I went back to Jamaica and got married. The immigration process took more than three years for my husband to join me in the United States. I honestly believed that once he got a job our financially situation would have changed for the better. We now had a one-bedroom apartment which cost more than my one room I occupied before he came. We also bought a tiny car and all I can remember was that it was white. It was nothing fancy as I cannot even remember the make or model. Clearly our expenditure grew, and my income remained the same. My darling husband was going out daily to look for employment to increase our earnings, but it took a while for him to land a job.

One day pulling up at the gas station with my car almost on empty with not one paper bill in my wallet and no credit or debit card. I had to count out the coins in my cup holder that amounted to a little over three dollars to put gas in my car. Embarrassed as I drove off with tears in my eyes. I desperately begged God for a breakthrough. I admitted to Him that I was freezing from the winter in my finances and if He could send me some warmth or rays of sunshine to get through this season. I promised I would show my gratitude to Him by serving Him for the rest of my life. My eagerness and last-ditch for a breakthrough in my finances had hit an all-time high.

During this cold frigid winter season, the temperature kept dropping and we had to cut back on many things to make ends meet. Not like we were living lavishly, this was a cut back from what was already the sparse essentials. We were willful about giving our tithes and from the gross because we believed every word in Malachi 3:8-12. We could not afford not to tithe as we trusted it to be our vehicle to a financial breakthrough, "*Will a man rob God? Yet ye have robbed me. But ye say, wherein have we robbed thee? In tithes and offerings. Ye are cursed with a curse: for ye have robbed me, even this whole nation. Bring ye all the tithes into the storehouse, that there may be meat in mine house, and prove me now herewith, saith the Lord of hosts, if I will not open you the windows of heaven, and pour you out a blessing, that there shall not be room enough to receive it.*" We wanted the double curse to be so far removed from us but more importantly we were anticipating the poured out over flowing blessing. It is so easy to get discouraged, entertain the

We could not afford not to tithe as we trusted it to be our vehicle to a financial breakthrough.

thoughts of giving up when things are not happening as quickly as we would like them to. I had to remind myself that God's timing is always perfect and that because I see little to no progress in my situation that does not mean He is not working on our behalf.

The tendency for some Christians when faced with financial struggles is to hold back on the giving of their tithes and offering. This is a trick and a plan of the enemy to further sink us in financial despair, by making us eat our seeds instead of sowing it. It is a huge mistake and a practice that should be shunned. If we believe the word of God, it clearly states that we are robbing God, and this will not yield a blessing. Why risk being double cursed, why not do the opposite and tithe your way out of the financial hardship? Do not allow the enemy and your fleshy desires to cause you to miss out on what God has in store for you.

Why risk being double cursed, why not do the opposite and tithe your way out of the financial hardship?

I believe that financial hardship can come upon us because of various reasons; some of which we have no control over. One of the things that we need to guard ourselves from as Christians is the spirit of discontent and covetousness. This can cause us to attempt to live like the Jones's and as the Jamaican colloquial expression states, *"putting our basket where our hands can't reach it."* Paul, the Apostle states that we should be content in whatsoever state we find ourselves. (Philippians 4:11). Little is much when God is in it. The widow in St Mark 12: 41 – 44 only had her two mites but she gave it all. It was her entire living. She did not withhold her giving to the Lord because of her current situation, instead she gave without reservations. She did not stop to evaluate what would happen to her after she gave her all. Her sustenance was of no concern to her, I believe this widow knew the source of her survival and that God would come through for her.

The Lord stayed true to His promises and rewarded our faithfulness in giving. Ian got a full-time role and our combined income made things a lot easier. Seven years into our marriage the Lord blessed us with our beautiful baby girl. Again, we found ourselves in a tight spot financially, but I believed that the God who brought us through before would be able to bring us out once more. Looking to Him as our source and the jobs as our resource kept us focus and grounded during this winter season. My will and determination to get over the dry daunting spells of winter forced me to secure a second job. I wanted my daughter to have everything she needed and more importantly I wanted a more long-term sustainability plan for our finance. I did not intend to sit around and complain about the scarceness of winter and what I did not have. Instead, I sought for ways to improve my financial status. I went looking for fleece and with every step asking God for divine guidance and financial wisdom.

Living in the United States of America now for over twenty – eight years I have experienced many occurrences of winter in my finances brought on by different reasons. Once I suffered from a broken ankle that had me out of work on disability for over six weeks which significantly reduced my take home pay. God exceeded our expectation during that winter season with the little we had by allowing us to purchase the home we are now living in. We could not afford the asking price and the Lord granted us favor that resulted in the owner significantly lowering the price. We were able to secure an affordable mortgage and make the down payment. To date we have not missed a payment and we have no one to thank but God. Truly He made a way when there was no way. It is important to note that winter has its benefits; it removes the leaves from the trees and makes things that were once hidden visible. Have you ever noticed how different the landscape looks when winter comes? With only one and a half salary, God allowed us to see that He was our Jehovah Jireh – The Lord who provides and not the job.

A few other occasions of winter in my finance was the downsizing of my job and as a result I was laid off. This created a huge reduction in our household income that left us having to make significant adjustment in our lifestyle. Also, an unexpected huge car repair for almost five thousand dollars. These circumstances plunged our finances into cold weather, but we were not in despair. Poor money management was also the culprit in some of my circumstances. Through it all I have learned to trust in Jesus. God's word served as a constant reminder and a source of strength when I was going through my financial crisis. I empowered and fueled myself with His word. He stated in Psalm 50:10, *"For every beast of the forest is mine, and the cattle upon a thousand hills."* I felt insulated from the negative degrees of the season by meditating on the word of God and His promises.

As the scriptures began to take root in my life, I practiced to not only repeat the word but to believe, live and act on the word. It was then I started to notice a consistent change in my financial situation. I would incorporate the scriptures in my prayer for example, *"Beloved, I wish above all things that thou mayest prosper and be in health, even as thy soul prospereth,"* (3 John 2:2). I had to put my faith in action because faith without works is dead. Murmuring and complaining was replaced with thanksgiving and worship. Every day for me became a day of thanksgiving. Realizing that death and life is in the power of the tongue, speaking life over my finances has now become a necessary practice. Decreeing and declaring that I was rich and that I had enough even when it was obvious that I was in the red, helped me to switch my focus. You must cultivate the attitude that like every other season, the winter in your finance is not permanent-it will pass. I also became a better steward of my finances as I asked God for financial wisdom in all things pertaining to money. Drawing on my experiences, I am now able to make better financial decisions.

One of the things to recall when struggling financially is that God cares for us and our needs are never overlooked or insignificant. He reminds us to, *"Take no thought for your life, what ye shall eat, or what ye shall drink; nor yet for your body, what ye shall put on. Is not the life more than meat, and the body than raiment? Behold the fowls of the air: for they sow not, neither do they reap, nor gather into barns; yet your heavenly Father feedeth them. Are ye not much better than they? Which of you by taking thought can add one cubit unto his stature? And why take ye thought for raiment? Consider the lilies of the field, how they grow; they toil not, neither do they spin: And yet I say unto you, that even Solomon in all his glory was not arrayed like one of these."* The lost son in St Luke 15: 11-32 perspective was permanently altered during the winter season of his finances when he came to himself and decided to go back home. He had lost everything, his entire inheritance, but he knew where to go for help. He arose and decided to go back home to his father. He was no longer willing to freeze in the less than favorable temperature he found himself in.

This young man had brought his financial winter upon himself by walking out of his father's presence and squandered his inheritance. Finding himself in such a low state that he would be pleased to eat what the pigs were eating. No doubt he was preserved by God and came to his senses so that he never had to get to that stage. No matter where you find yourself financially if you commit your ways to Him He will take care of you like the fowls of the air and the lilies of the field. Financial success for the child of God looks somewhat different, it is not necessarily having a huge bank account or huge investment. It is really being good stewards over what God has blessed us with. The wise use of our resources to glorify God. You may be feeling the harshness of winter in your finance which was brought on by a divorce, lost in your 401K, unexpected job loss, death of a spouse, sickness or the stock market crashed and wiped out your entire savings. Christ, like the father in the story of the lost son has bread enough to feed all His hired servants, please allow Him to pour you out a blessing. Do not be afraid to accept the coat He has given you to provide warmth as you go through this chilly season. It is only a matter of time before your spring is here.

Today, I am better equipped to manage my finances based on the lessons I have learned along the way. My winter experiences allowed me to gain financial awareness and intelligence. I now evaluate each situation to see what got me in this season in the first place. In one of my financial winter seasons I did an inventory of my credit card balances. The accumulative balance was ridiculously high, and I had nothing substantial to show for it. I called up the banks and made payment arrangements. In that moment I discarded all my credit cards. Upon completion of the payments, I closed out all my credit card accounts. I no longer see the need to do everything everyone else is doing. If it is not in my budget, then it is not affordable. I have learned to simplify areas of my life by staying in my lane. This helped me tremendously to avert some of the self-induced financial winters I have had in the past. With no credit card at my disposal I can only purchase the things that I can immediately afford, and I no longer wrestle with the temptation to charge it!

Let me stress that we cannot insulate ourselves from all financial winters but for those that can be avoided let us work towards doing so. To help prevent financial winters one should create a budget, shop off the clearance rack, cut coupons, wait for the sales, go thrifting and improvise where you can, live below your means, pay off your debt, start an emergency fund and stick to what you promise you would do. Even if you fall off a few weeks or months it is okay, just continue where you left off. Decide on what your spending and saving goals are and intentionally work towards it. Benefits of budgeting include providing "guardrails" (i.e., designated limits) for spending, achieving financial goals and above everything else for your own peace of mind.

Today, when I experience winter in my finance I can depend on God because He will NEVER let me beg for bread or suffer. I believe that if it means sending manna from above, He will bring me out. If I must borrow vessels, pour oil and sell to appease the creditors like the widow in 2 Kings 4: 1 – 7, He will provide. I can rejoice because I am confident that this too will pass. His grace is sufficient to keep me because He promised to supply all my needs according to His riches in glory by Christ Jesus. (Philippians

4:19). He will not let His children come into reproach and ridicule. When Jesus and Peter had to pay the temple taxes they had no money, but He knew the fish that had the coin. He told Peter, "*Notwithstanding, lest we should offend them, go thou to the sea, and cast an hook, and take up the fish that first cometh up; and when thou hast opened his mouth, thou shalt find a piece of money: that take, and give unto them for me and thee,*" (St. Matthew 17:27). The coin was enough to meet both their needs. One coin was all it took! What a mighty God we serve! He will bring you out of your financial winter by allowing ONE coin to work for you.

God is bigger than our financial crises, so place it before Him and watch Him bring about a change in your situation. Stop and look at every spending decision as a spiritual decision; being good stewards over what God has entrusted to us will allow us to seek Him about our spending choices, and I am sure that will have us doing so much better in our finances. Also, be wise to seek godly counsel as you reorganize your finances. Find someone who can give you practical advice and hold you accountable on reorienting your priorities. Remember that the key to stewardship is found in our attitude toward God and what He's given us. All that we have belongs to Him and for His glory. Once God has brought you out of the winter of finance and while you cannot encase yourself from future winter, you can better prepare for it by:

- Developing a monthly budget that includes a strategy for getting out of debt.
- Utilize a strategy for saving and investing.
- Consistently giving back to the Lord.
- Using cash whenever possible.

Whatever you do try not to become a pessimist. See your glass ALWAYS as half full instead of half empty. It does make a huge difference. Your harvest is coming. Remember winter is necessary for a GREAT harvest!

Focus Scriptures

"But seek ye first the kingdom of God, and his righteousness; and all these things shall be added unto you." **(St. Matthew 6:33).**

"Owe no man anything, but to love one another: for he that loveth another hath fulfilled the law." **(Romans 13:8).**

"Will a man rob God? Yet ye have robbed me. But ye say, wherein have we robbed thee? In tithes and offerings. Ye are cursed with a curse: for ye have robbed me, even this whole nation. Bring ye all the tithes into the storehouse, that there may be meat in mine house, and prove me now herewith, saith the Lord of hosts, if I will not open you the windows of heaven, and pour you out a blessing, that there shall not be room enough to receive it. And I will rebuke the devourer for your sakes, and he shall not destroy the fruits of your ground; neither shall your vine cast her fruit before the time in the field, saith the Lord of hosts. And all nations shall call you blessed: for ye shall be a delightsome land, saith the Lord of hosts. **(Malachi 3:8-12).**

"Honour the LORD with thy substance, and with the firstfruits of all thine increase." **(Proverbs 3:9).**

"The rich ruleth over the poor, and the borrower [is] servant to the lender." **(Proverbs 22:7).**

"He that hath pity upon the poor lendeth unto the LORD; and that which he hath given will he pay him again." **(Proverbs 19:17).**

"Be thou diligent to know the state of thy flocks, [and] look well to thy herds." **(Proverbs 27:23).**

"Give, and it shall be given unto you; good measure, pressed down, and shaken together, and running over, shall men give into your bosom. For with the same measure that ye mete withal it shall be measured to you again." **(St. Luke 6:38).**

CHAPTER THREE

Career

Before migrating to the United States, I had completed college and held several jobs. I had taught high school for one year, but really did not like the take home work of grading papers and lesson plans etc. I had also worked with the Ministry of Health for about six months. My final job before migrating was with the country's Telephone Company as a Data Analyst. I really loved this job and was totally saddened when I got my visa to migrate. The air of independence I felt as a young working adult was very liberating, and I did not want to give that up for something that was uncertain. Nevertheless, my immediate family was migrating, so I was left with no choice. I had to pack up and relocate.

I had my degree in Nutrition and Dietetics, and when I came to the United States of America I was told that to work as a Dietician I would have to go back to college and become certified. Vehemently, I dismissed that idea because I was upset with the system. I knew I was qualified to do the job. I trusted God for guidance and I asked Him to help me to humble myself as it related to my career. With that said, I took a job at the hospital as a Dietary clerk. It was a role was way below my credentials, but I did it with excellence. This role allowed me the opportunity to interact with the patients, and the moments for witnessing about my Savior were many. The chances to share my faith fueled my love for the job even though it was only per diem and slightly above minimum wage. Believing that, *"The steps of a good man are ordered by the Lord: and he delighteth in his way,"* (Psalm 37:23), I looked at this role as a stepping stone to the bigger things that God had in store for me. I believed Him to take control of my steps as I prayerfully followed where He led.

After a few years, I left the hospital to work as the Food Service Director of a private Nursing Home for ten years. This job was an awesome blessing as the schedule allowed me the flexibility to attend my church services and all my church events. It could not have gotten any better; the employees were cooperative; the residents were a delight and I enjoyed what I did. It was during that time that I gave birth to my first and only child – Sanian. This job had become a definite comfort zone because of my tenure and role. I had five weeks of vacation, three weeks of sick time and that did not include holidays. My daughter became the recipient of these vacation days when she was sick or just needed to be picked up early. In all this, I gave God thanks for being such a Waymaker. Our needs were met, and we were contented.

Approaching my tenth year at the Nursing Home, I became restless in the role and thought it was a good time for me to move on to do something different. I applied for a role as a Customer Service agent with a subsidiary of a newspaper company and within several months I became a part of the leadership team. The interaction with training and developing the agents served as a reward for me because I absolutely love teaching and imparting knowledge. Work for me at the Call Center was like living out my God given purpose. I not only had the opportunity to coach and make a difference in my role I was hired for, but I was also able to minister to souls. I also invited them to church and a few of them even surrendered their lives to Christ. The monetary compensation was not that great but the satisfaction that I received from witnessing was exhilarating. The zeal of a few of my agents to know more about Christ convinced me to start a cell group ministry in my home. We would meet on Thursdays to discuss the word of God and fellowship. I was determined to let Christ be known beyond the walls. I was not afraid to let them know about the Apostolic lifestyle. I was enjoying my job and the effectual ministry door that was opened for me.

Life was good! I had a job that allowed us to live comfortably and enabled us to afford the things we needed. We lived in a fair to fine neighborhood, we were able to eat out at our leisure; our daughter was enrolled in music, swimming and tennis lessons and we were able to vacation a minimum of twice per year. Unfortunately, one day this came to a screeching halt. Winter showed up; creating major setbacks in our well laid out financial plans. "Why now and what was I going to do?" It was business as usual, I woke up and did my morning routine which involved my morning devotion acknowledging my Maker. I believed that in ALL our ways we should acknowledge God and allow Him to direct our path. I got my daughter ready for school and then headed to the office. This morning, the traffic was so heavy that I made my exit two exits earlier to avoid the bumper to bumper scenario. Finally, I made it to the office and gave God thanks for His journeying mercies and His travelling grace.

As customary, I started the morning going through those emails that came in after I had left the office the previous day. Most of the emails were FYI's, however, there was this one invite for a 10:00 am meeting with the CEO of my company and all other employees on my management level. This was an unusual surprise because meetings of that nature are usually made known to us in advance to ensure the attendance of everyone involved. Being one of the managers that had a later start time, the office was already buzzing with speculations as to the reason for this urgent meeting. There were a lot of ideas ranging from, "the business was folding under," "strategic plans for the upcoming quarter," "changes our client required in our performance," and the list kept on growing.

Management and employees were gathered in groups whispering among themselves. The longest two-hour period for me that day was from 8:00 am – 10:00 am. I sat at my desk with my personal speculations that I was too afraid to share, fearing that it might just be the reality. At approximately five minutes to 10:00 am other managers along with myself began filing into the dedicated conference room to secure our seats. The look of uncertainty, confusion and anticipation was noticeable on all the faces. The room grew still as everyone awaited the arrival of upper management and the CEO to make their grand entrance. They greeted everyone with the usual, "Good morning, how is everyone doing?" A few persons muttered "fine," reluctantly. The CEO went straight to the heart of the matter. At this point, we were told that everyone on my management level positions and the department that we managed would be eliminated in a matter of months. They were moving the entire operations out of State. The offer on the table was those who were interested in relocating could keep their jobs at a lower salary.

The room grew silent as everyone avoided eye contact with each other. The explanation they gave for the elimination of positions was that one of their largest clients had decided to take their business elsewhere, and they would no longer be able to afford the operating cost. The apologies began to flow and so did the tears of most of my colleagues. The end date was given which allowed me at least six months to make the transition. During this whole process, I sat engulfed in my own world thinking about my personal situation followed by the aged old question, "What am I going to do?" My thoughts raced; I had spent a decade at this company and now the curtains were coming down involuntarily. Fear of tomorrow gripped my thoughts. Winter had reared its head in my career, but then came the comforting voice from within, *"For we know that all things work together for the good to them who love God to those who are the called according to His purpose,"* (Romans 8:28). That was my queue to demonstrate what I have been preaching and teaching others for years as a minister of the Gospel. I needed to look straight into the face of this adversity called job loss and KNOW that God is ABLE!

After the announcement, my management team demonstrated some compassion, stating that employees who were not in a state of mind to work for the rest of the day were at liberty to leave the office. Being strengthened by the word of God, I stayed for the entire day knowing that Jesus does all things well. This was my winter to trust in the promises of the God I professed and magnified to be a Waymaker. There was not much accomplished in terms of work because my day was spent being a sounding board for many who needed to vent and cry. I left the office with mixed emotions, not sure if I should be happy or sad. Was it time for me to move on or was this a premature discharge? The fear of the how the bills were going to be paid captivated my thoughts on the drive home that evening.

Breaking the news to my husband and daughter was hard, nevertheless I did it with a sense of assurance that God would take care of us. The support I received from friends and family members was incredible and this made the load of my pending unemployment much easier to bear. The journey from unemployment to re-employment had some bumps in the road, some expected and some unexpected. There were moments of despair, fear of the unknown and much anticipation, but within all that mixed emotions there was always that deep settled peace that God was still in control and His promises were still authentic.

Losing a job is rarely seen as a good thing, especially since financial pressures can cause tremendous tension in a marriage and family. Often, I would do a temperature check with my husband because he was now the sole bread winner. One day he said to me, "Sandra relax, you are not going to be out of a job for the rest of your life." He wanted me to enjoy the moment and not stress. It felt humanly impossible for me to do but with God it was possible. One evening about six months into my unemployment, I felt so down and devalued. I was allowing the absence of a job to define who I was. I felt so sad and broken. I remember standing in the bathroom looking in the mirror and asking God, "Why me?" I begged Him to make a way and come through for me. Standing there, the Lord gave me the title for the book, "Overcoming Job Loss - A Spiritual Guide. I began questioning the Lord by asking Him, "How can I write this book and I was still unemployed and what would be my point of reference? The Lord gave me insights of what should be contained in the book. Today, the book is published with six faith-based principles that I lived by during my period of unemployment.

I had to believe that God sees the bigger picture and that He opens one door and closes another. Psalm 75:6 – 7 states, *"For promotion cometh neither from the east, nor from the west, nor from the south. But God is the judge: he putteth down one, and setteth up another."* I had to embrace the word of God and trust Him with my career because He knows how my story will end. In the winter of your career, do not stay under the covers and resign to doom and gloom. Better days are still ahead. There is no area in our life that God is not willing to help. We must believe this-He has our best interest at heart! He did not take away our job because He had nothing better to do. I know this might be hard to digest but in the plan of God it was time for us to move on. Unfortunately, our limited knowledge of the future makes us unable to see God's best laid out plans for us. God is not a liar; in fact, it is impossible for Him to lie. (Hebrews 6:18). He stated in His Words that He has good plans for you. (Jeremiah 29:1).

In the winter of your career, do not stay under the covers and resign to doom and gloom. Better days are still ahead.

The loss of your job can result in bitterness if you do not guard yourself against the negative feelings that enter your thoughts. Your bitterness can stem from the fact that you think that you were dealt with unfairly. After all you did your job to the best of your ability and you gave 110%. The story of Joseph is a great illustration of letting go of bad feelings and love in spite of. Joseph did not pretend that what his brothers did to him was not evil; it most certainly was. He knew the intent of their hearts was to get rid of him. Joseph saw deeper than their intentions and despite what they were doing, God was doing something far more wonderful.

Yes, they sinned against Joseph, but God used their sins to accomplish His eternal plan. In Genesis 50:20, Joseph looked back on thirty years of trial mixed with triumph and acknowledged God's hand in every detail of his life. Joseph knew that the hatred, betrayal, slavery, imprisonment, loneliness and separation, were all part of a much bigger plan. God used the valleys and the victories of Joseph's life to reach Joseph's brothers, to encourage Jacob; to bring the children of Israel into Egypt, and to literally save the nation of Israel. Surely, God meant it for good! However, we can be sure of one thing, as we pass through this life, and that is we can count on the fact that every valley and every victory is a part of His perfect plan. For us, God will use them all for our good and for His glory! That is His promise.

We would have to admit that we like the victories more than we like the valleys. We like the good days more than we like the bad days. Here is the question that confronts us: are we willing to joyfully endure everything life throws at us knowing that God is behind it all and that He will get glory from it? Are we willing to accept His will, even when it goes against our will, knowing that He will develop us through it? As we pass through the hard places of life, it is easy to forget that God is in control. The next time life pulls the rug out from under your feet, remember that God is always there to catch you. The highs and lows I experienced during the winter months of job loss resulted in a stronger more consistent prayer life for me. The more I prayed, the more my faith began to rise. Where I was doubting, I began to trust again. Where I was confused, God gave me clarity. Where I was anxious, God stood as my Prince of Peace.

It was during these moments that He really taught my heart to smile again and my feet to dance amid my loss and hardship. The Psalmist David reminded me, "*The lines are fallen unto me in pleasant places; yea, I have a goodly heritage. I will bless the Lord, who hath given me counsel: my reins also instruct me in the night seasons. I have set the Lord always before me: because he is at my right hand, I shall not be moved,"* (Psalm 16: 6-8). My situation did not change immediately but my outlook did. The more I trusted Him, the more I found myself the benefactor of a deep settled peace. Desperately wanting the Lord to be pleased with me, I also employed an attitude of thanksgiving and gratefulness. I developed unchanging reasons for my gratitude-my thanksgiving was not predicated on the blessings that I received from the Lord. Instead, it was birthed out of the fact that God is sovereign and that He never changes. Circumstances change but God does not.

Winter serves as a time of rest and replenishing for trees and vegetation so that they can produce more succulent and tastier crops. My state of unemployment became a perfect time for me to sharpen my existing skills and gain new ones. I am a firm believer that one cannot know too much. You might have been in a position at your former job where you did everything manually. For example, an accountant who only worked with an excel spreadsheet, now would be the perfect time for you to learn the software applications that serve as industry standards for that specific discipline. During the time I was home, I took classes to obtain my Project Management Certification (PMP) and was successful in passing the five-hour examination. Sharpening or advancing my skills not only placed me on the cutting edge but significantly set me above other prospective job seekers and increased my earning power. The Bible states in 1 Chronicles 12:32, *"And of the children of Issachar, which were men that had understanding of the times, to know what Israel ought to do; the heads of them were two hundred; and all their brethren were at their commandment."* These men did well because they understood the times. This gave them an advantage over their peers.

Ten months into my job loss, the Lord provided a job for me at a Fortune 500 company. The job was better than the previous roles I held both in monetary compensation and benefits. During the interviewing process, I recall taking a manila envelope that had the documents for the new role with me to our seven day fast daily. I would pray over the package and ask God if it was His will for me to have the role He should make everything go smoothly and if not show me a sign. Acknowledging Him in my career choice was of paramount importance this go around. At times we get stuck in careers because that was the hand that was dealt to us, but this time, I needed Him to be an integral part of the decision making. I wanted a job that provided me the flexibility to continue doing the work of the Lord without restrictions and the job did just that.

However, about six months into the job, I began to experience some challenges with an immediate supervisor. Oh no I thought, this could not be happening. I believed that this job was answered prayers. Sinking in despair and distress, the enemy wanted me to doubt that God gave me this job. This individual was like a thorn in the flesh and criticized and nitpicked at my performance. I was given no room for errors; it was a new role and the mentoring and shadowing opportunity was only for a few days. Mine was cut short. Frustrated by the way I was being treated, I remember driving home praying and asking God for directives. As I began to pray, the tears came rolling down my cheeks – to say I was feeling overwhelmed, is an understatement. At that moment I said, "Lord I thought this was the job you gave me, why am I going through this turbulence?"

A part of me wanted to quit immediately. I did not feel like I could go through this constant scrutiny. I needed to be in a place where I could thrive and look forward to going to work. For months I suffered in silence because I had testified beyond doubt that God gave me this job. How could I now go back and complain about the blessings that I had received from His hand? This I thought would have made me an unbeliever. One day while at work I felt challenged by the workload and I decided to take a break and go to the bathroom to pray. In a total moment of truth, I confessed to God that I could not do this anymore and I was not happy.

As I stood in the bathroom stall trying to figure out how I was going to leave this job, the Holy Spirit instructed me to call one of my confidants.

With new found strength, I went back on the floor and found an office that offered me the privacy needed to make the phone call. I shared with my confidant what I had been experiencing for the past months. She provided me step by step guidance on how to handle the situation. A little nervous to carry out the steps but prayerfully and with strength from God I did. My situation was investigated, and the individual was removed from being my immediate supervisor. I was now blessed and favored to have someone who respected my work and was instrumental in my promotion and merit increase. Through all of this, I learned a valuable lesson. Winter does not give you the rights to throw in the towel and curl up and die. Every leaf may have fallen from the tree and you might be exposed to extreme cold that has left you frost bitten and shaken but whatever you do, do not quit. I had to demonstrate resilience and continued to show up even when I did not feel like it.

Winter does not give you the rights to throw in the towel and curl up and die. Every leaf may have fallen from the tree and you might be exposed to extreme cold that has left you frost bitten and shaken but whatever you do, do not quit.

This was a test of my faith and my trust in God; I honestly knew that God had provided this job for me, but the enemy wanted me to abort my blessing because of a wintery experience. Many days I had to wrap myself in the warmth of the blessed assurance I had in Christ. Remember, doubt is an enemy to faith because it speaks with a voice that challenges the truth or the reliability of what we should believe. To overcome doubt, we must fill our minds with the word of God, meditating deeply and repetitively on it. Doubt is the evidence of an unconsecrated heart and mind. This is a lack of devotion to God's word and like fear, it torments. Choosing to believe God is a decision I had to make regardless of what my situation looked like. My faith eventually yielded fruits of blessing that I am enjoying today. Do not let the snow get in your shoes causing you to come to a standstill and cripple you. Keep moving because it is in moving that you become warm and able to stay the course.

Focus Scriptures

"Trust in the Lord with all thine heart; and lean not unto thine own understanding. In all thy ways acknowledge him, and he shall direct thy paths. "In all thy ways acknowledge him, and he shall direct thy paths." **(Proverbs 3: 5-6).**

"For I know the thoughts that I think toward you, saith the LORD, thoughts of peace, not of evil to give you an expected end." **(Jeremiah 29:11).**

"I will instruct thee and teach thee in the way which thou shalt go: I will guide thee with mine eye." **(Psalm 32:8).**

"Commit thy works unto the LORD, and thy thoughts shall be established." **(Proverbs 16:3).**

"There are many devices in a man's heart; nevertheless the counsel of the LORD, that shall stand." **(Proverbs19:21).**

"Delight thyself also in the LORD; and he shall give thee the desires of thine heart." **(Psalm 37:4).**

"Prepare thy work without and make it fit for thyself in the field; and afterwards build thine house." **(Proverbs 24:27).**

"Blessed [is] the man that trusteth in the LORD, and whose hope the LORD is." **(Jeremiah 17:7).**

"John answered and said, A man can receive nothing, except it be given him from heaven." **(St. John 3:27).**

"A man's gift maketh room for him, and bringeth him before great men." **(Proverbs 18:16).**

"Every good gift and every perfect gift is from above, and cometh down from the Father of lights, with whom is no variableness, neither shadow of turning." **(James 1:17).**

CHAPTER FOUR

Relationships

"And above all things have fervent charity among yourselves: for charity shall cover the multitude of sins." 1 Peter 4:8

As a child I learned the song, "No man is an island,
No man stands alone,
Each man's joy is joy to me,
Each man's grief is my own."

I honestly did not know the full meaning of this song until much later in life. Nothing is more important than the relationships in our lives. I would dare to even say that relationship is a gift from God that He has blessed us all with, to make our lives better. When God created the world, He then stooped down and created man from the dust of the earth and blew in him the breath of life and man became a living soul. (Genesis 2:7). Although God created the sea creatures, birds' animals, and all kinds of living things, He knew they could not connect with Adam. In Genesis 2:18, God said it was not good for man to be alone and made provision for that aloneness.

This act of God amplifies the fact that He did not intend for us to do life on our own or to be lonely. After establishing that fact, the Bible states that He created a woman, who was called Eve to be Adam's help meet. God commanded them to be fruitful, multiply and replenish the earth. (Genesis 1:28). The importance of relationship was further seen in the life of Jesus Christ. He was born in a family. He had a mother, father, brother and sisters. He not only had followers, but He had friends, one named Lazarus. When Lazarus died the Bible recorded in St John 11:35, *"Jesus wept."* This verse is said to be the shortest verse in the Bible, but more importantly it is a verse that shows the loving, caring human side of the God that we serve. Lazarus was His friend. They had a relationship, and He would spend time in their home, eating, laughing and sharing. Isn't that how we feel when someone that we have a relationship dies? It leaves us hurting and sad.

Relationships are more than just someone that you are related to by blood, or by name change in marriage or adoption etc. It is not that social media status that is void of any kind of interaction except liking each other's posts and becoming a follower of that page. If someone who was following your social media page dies, most likely you would not be mourning them the way you would a loved one. You may show some form of sympathy but nothing deep rooted, because you were never really in a relationship with that individual. To be in a relationship one must be interconnected with each other, nothing superficial. One must be totally committed. Not distant and separated in our own worlds. It is possible that people can be surrounded by other people in a crowded setting, and not experience community. We can be a part of a company, a club, or an assembly and not feel that sense of belonging or acceptance. We can carpool, share an office, and even a home and not have significant relationships.

Across the span of my life, I have been blessed to experience some meaningful relationships. These interactions provided for me a safe base where I can be transparent and share my opinions, feelings, woes and joys. For me, that is important. In these relationships I do not feel judged or looked down upon because of something I did or said. Notice, I did not say corrected. Individuals that have your best interest at heart will at times have to correct you in love. Condoning wrong is not a mark of a healthy connection. Jesus loved His disciples, but He had to call them out on their fear and unbelief. *"And he saith unto them, why are ye fearful, O ye of little faith? Then he arose, and rebuked the winds and the sea; and there was a great calm,"* (St. Matthew 8:26).

To date, I am still enjoying and basking in relationships that I have held dear for over thirty years. Let me hasten to add that it was not always easy to maintain these relationships. My relationships have seen their fair share of ups, downs, and hurdles in the road. Sometimes, I could hear the screeching halts coming and the three strikes you are out weighing in on my relationships. On the flip side, I have had some relationships that did not survive the winter season. Others that are currently going through the season, with the hope that they will survive. There are different situations that can bring winter in a relationship-lack of trust, disloyalty, the busyness of life, death, finances, cheating, different interests. This by no means an absolute list; there are so many other factors that can plunge a relationship in the winter season.

Death is a major the major element that shatters relationships and brings about finality in both physical and emotional ties. One other such relationship was that of my brother Ken, who died tragically. His death occurred on April 28, 1990, when he was gunned down by the hands of violent men. Ken was the ideal brother; he was our protector growing up in the island of Jamaica. He always ensured that the boys on the corner stayed away from us. There was nothing that he had that was too good to share or give to us.

Ken migrated to the United States of American to join our mother years before we did. As an older brother he would make it his priority to guarantee that we got our Christmas and birthday cards. yearly. Tucked inside these cards would be a sizeable amount of US dollars, to ensure we had a good time. We were always happy for these gifts. To me he was the IDEAL older brother. His joyful demeanor and zest for life made him fun to be around. His untimely death not only shocked our family and caused deep rooted grief, but we are still left with scars and a shattered sibling relationship we all held dear. My mom was so broken, and grief stricken by his death that she would spend days just sitting and staring out the window without eating. Ken did everything for her and now that relationship was no more. Winter had brought death to this relationship, and we were all affected by it.

Interceding for my family during this season was the only thing I could do successfully. Nothing else worked as everyone was so sad. I encouraged them to draw on the strength that only God could give. Remembering the positive aspects of the life we shared with him would often eased the pain. Those memories are golden, and we will forever carry them with us in our hearts. For us to move on and continue to live, even after this broken relationship, we had to accept the loss and adjust to the environment without our brother Ken. The love and mercies of God brought us through just like He had promised in His word. It stated that He would bind up the broken hearted. "*The Spirit of the Lord God is upon me; because the Lord hath anointed me to preach good tidings unto the meek; he hath sent me to bind up the brokenhearted, to proclaim liberty to the captives, and the opening of the prison to them that are bound,*" (Isaiah 61:1). My brother's death brought meaning to our existence because it reminds us how precious life is and that we should cherish every moment we have with each other. The truth is, we never know when death is going to come and separate us from the relationship with our loved ones.

There is no way that I could speak about winter in my relationships without first mentioning the death of my beloved mother, Christina Mathilda Sterling – Salmon. With tears in my eyes, I still miss her to this very day. Even though it has been seventeen years. The loss of that winter still resides with me. During moments of deep sadness and perplexities, I wish I could reach for my phone and hear her familiar voice, *"Lorr take it one day at time."* Or the moments of joy and celebration when I knew she would be so proud of me and my accomplishments. However, God had a better plan for her when He promoted her to glory!

I vividly recall, Ian and I had just purchased our home and we were still in the process of settling in. It was one August afternoon that my eldest sister called me to inform me that my mom was diagnosed with stomach cancer, and it was at the end stage. She said the doctors were giving her three months. In disbelief and shock at what I was hearing at the other end of the line, the hot tears began to roll down my cheeks. In that moment, I was at a loss for words. When I finally got it together, I began shooting off questions after questions to my sister, who for the most part did not have the answers. I hung up the phone and knelt by the couch I was sitting on. I remember asking God to heal her just for me. Weak and upset from the news, I got up and called my mom. The minute she heard my voice she responded, *"Lorr it is true, but I will be fine."* Her composure and faith in God provided me with the strength to get through our conversation.

My mom lived in Massachusetts and I lived in New Jersey, but I spoke to my mom EVERYDAY. (This was after she got over her initial shock of me moving to New Jersey after migrating in the United States for only two weeks). Sometimes it was just a quick check in and other times we spoke for hours depending on the topic of discussion. These lengthy conversations were usually about my siblings J. I believe that I was my mother's confidant. My siblings might disagree when they read this book, but that was how my mom made me feel. I would look forward to our interactions and laughter; she was also my confidant and someone whose strength and resilience I admired. My mom raised all her eleven children pretty much on her own. That kind of strength and tenacity pushed me to do well in school-not only to make her proud but to ensure that I would not have to manually work as hard as she did. My mom was a dedicated and hard worker.

The effects of her diagnosis changed our daily dialogue; my mom became weak and had to be hospitalized. She was later transferred to a hospice and finally moved back home where we converted her bedroom to a hospital room. During the time of her brief illness, I must admit that my faith was shaken. Immersing myself in fasting and prayer for extended periods, desperately attempting to regain my trust in God. Partnering with other intercessors for her healing was also a part of my regular cadence during her illness. I begged God to let her live for my sake. Living in New Jersey was very rough for me. I wanted to see my mom, to hold her hand, and give her whatever she wanted. A part of me would have loved to quit my job and move back home to be closer to her. I knew this was unrealistic, and above all my mom would not have agreed. My sister Kaye had now become my primary liaison to my mom and would give me updates about her daily condition. These phone calls would end leaving me feeling discouraged and upset with God as her health was rapidly declining.

In my vulnerable state, I even went as far as making a promise to God. I told Him if He did this for me, I would not ask Him for anything else. This was a final attempt to get God to work in my favor. Distraught and wanting to see my mom more often, I requested a schedule change on my job. This was unheard of in a Call Center environment. However, God favored me. I was able to work Monday – Friday, allowing me the weekends off to go visit my mom in Massachusetts. The yearning to hear her feeble voice and words of encouragement served as the fuel I needed to take the trip weekly. I interject here to say, thanks to individuals that I had meaningful relationships with. They understood my pain and would do anything to help ease it. A dear friend of mine was one such individual. She became my personal chauffeur from Massachusetts to New Jersey when my husband was unable to take me. For me, that was a demonstration of love, care and concern. Stace I am forever grateful!

As I watched my mom's quality of life deteriorated, and she was no longer able to communicate, I could feel the winter easing its way in our relationship. The absence of her reassuring voice brought a deep sadness and fear within me. My visits were spent at her bedside along with my other siblings. Reminiscing about our childhood and talks about how courageous and strong she was. During those moments, I felt feelings of anger and disappointment towards God. Questions like how could He do this to me, why wasn't God healing her? What did I have to do to get His attention and what would life be without the relationship with my mother? These questions consistently plagued my mind. My faith began to waiver and so did my prayers. Some days I felt like it was useless to pray. God wasn't answering me anyway.

Early morning, on October 31, 2001 my mom transitioned this life. The news of her death was gut wrenching and heart breaking. I felt like I had lost everything-including my hope. One of the bravest things I had to do in all my life was mustering up the strength for my siblings as we prepared for her Celebration of Life service. I placed my feelings and emotions aside until we laid her to rest peacefully. Upon returning home to New Jersey, the feeling of being let down by God was overwhelming and left me in despair. One day, while talking with a pastor friend who was checking in on me, I shared with Him how despondent and discouraged I felt about God not healing my mother. In my ranting, I made the statement, "the drug addicts are still living, and they have no purpose, they should be the ones dying." Immediately, he stopped me and softly said, "Sandy they are not saved, your mom was baptized, filled with the Holy Ghost and ready to meet her Savior. These addicts need a chance to make it right."

For the very first time during this three-month ordeal, I was able to view my mom's death through a different lens. I wanted the Lord to heal her so badly for my selfish reason. I wanted our wonderful mother-daughter relationship to continue. Winter had come, and our relationship did not survive it. In the days ahead, I asked God to forgive me for my negative reaction and to increase my faith and trust in Him. Grappling with the loss of this relationship allowed me to turn to the God of all comfort. I had to find a way to bow to His sovereign will, because I recognized that His plans trump my faith. *"For my thoughts are not your thoughts, neither are your ways my ways, saith the LORD.* (Isaiah 55:8). I had to release the hurt, disappointment and pain that I was feeling to receive His comfort. After all, He is the God of all comfort and He wanted to help me get through this chilling season.

I had to recognize that I needed others to truly heal and move beyond grief. Self-pity and every other destructive emotion serve to sink us deeper in isolation and depression. When exposed to the joy of others, the negative effects of grief begin to die. Like a mold does when it is exposed to light. If the enemy can cut us off from others, then it's like a wolf separating a sheep from the flock, making us easy preys. The rock-solid relationships that I had helped me tremendously during that season of my life. They offered me consolation in the word of God and some individuals were physically present to do fun things with me. These served as sources of good distractions. Putting all our tragedies into the perspective of eternity also minimizes their impact on us. All tragedies will be totally forgotten in eternity as we experience the comfort of the Lord in full measure. Romans 8:18 says, *"For I reckon that the sufferings of this present time are not worthy to be compared with the glory which shall be revealed in us."*

Meaningful relationships make our hearts glad and joyful; they provide support and camaraderie and give us all kind of support to help carry us through life's difficulties. However, when there are misunderstandings within our relationships, we may find ourselves feeling at a loss for what to do. I think most of us could say that relationships can be the best and the worst thing that can happen to us. A relationship can be a stress reliever on many occasions, but sadly, during misunderstandings, they can create much inner turmoil. When you open yourself to be in a relationship be it marriage, friendship, or parenting you are also opening yourself to pain and hurt. Love makes one vulnerable and unmasked, sharing the most intimate parts of who you are. There can be no honest relationship without this element of transparency.

Another way that winter shows up in relationships is the lack of reciprocity which manifests itself in some of the following ways: caring, commitment, communication, trust, love, time, authenticity, and concern. To cultivate and maintain a wholesome relationship one must put in the work. One cannot expect a thriving and budding relationship if there is no nurturing. Do not take your relationships lightly. We must do more than just reach out to others; we must share our lives with others as well. This should be a two-way approach-no one party should always be giving and no one party should always be taking. Reciprocity should be the precursor to any significant relationship. In its absence, we experience winter that can show itself in a myriad of ways. It is not enough to admit we need each other, or say, "Oh, a few friends would be nice." We must commit ourselves to getting beneath the surface talk. This should be more that the everyday pleasantries, and the frivolous, "I love you." Interest and accountability must be demonstrated to each other. Authenticity occurs when the masks come off, conversations get deep, hearts get vulnerable, lives are shared, accountability is invited, and tenderness flows. Believers in the body of Christ should behave like brothers and sisters. There must be the need for assimilation. Assimilation is becoming absorbed in the lives of others as an active participant, relating to, sharing with, and caring for others.

I have had the experience of winter showing up in one of my cherished relationships because of what I thought was lack of care and concern. This was someone that I loved and cared for, and our friendship existed for over a decade. It was that kind of friendship where we could complete each other's sentences effortlessly, so go figure. We spent countless hours together, confided in each other, laughed and cried together. This person saw me at my highest and my lowest. At one of the lowest points in my life my friend was not there for me. Feelings of sadness and dismay crowded my emotional space. Not only was I struggling with a severe loss, but I also had to deal with the pain and disappointment that I felt from the absence of my friend when I needed her most.

For me, winter showed itself in withdrawal and unforgiveness. I kept wondering what could be more important to my friend that caused her not to show up for me. Honestly, I tried many times to rationalize her behavior. However, through my lens I could not find a justifiable reason for her action. I took solace in the scripture, *"A friend loveth at all times, and a brother is born for adversity,"* (Proverbs 17:17). I used this scripture to justify my action. What made it worst was others who I had no relationship expressed their support, and here was someone I had invested in turned out to be a, "no show" for me. Days turned into weeks, weeks turned into months, and months turned into years as the gap in our relationship began to widen. On occasion when we saw each other it was a quick hello and we were both on our way. In the beginning the adjustment was hard, but with time it became the norm for both of us.

If we are not careful and acknowledge the Lord in our relationships, when winter comes we will allow it to kill the love, care and concern we have for each other. I had a huge part to play in this breaking down of a once cherished relationship because I allowed my feelings and justification to be the primary focus. Looking back, I should have QUICKLY demonstrated understanding and forgiveness! I should have somehow spent some more time understanding the reason for the action on the individual's part. Understanding only develops over time. It's based on knowledge. You understand others by seeing life from their perspective. It involves a tremendous amount of communication — of asking, sharing and listening.

Lack of forgiveness and pent up emotions erect barriers in our relationships which we will never be able to move beyond. Once you refuse to forgive you build a wall that cannot be penetrated. It then becomes impossible for the relationship to go further. Intimacy cannot progress, and trust is undermined. If we choose to hold the past against an individual, we are choosing to forfeit any opportunity for a deeper connection. Concerning the relationship mentioned, years later we met and discussed everything in detail and decided to salvage what was left of the relationship. The road ahead was long, but we were able to make it work. Instead of using the scripture, "a friend loveth at all times," (Proverbs 17:17), to support my action, I should have used it to help me to forgive and move on sooner.

Relationships can be risky. The choice to have a meaningful, lasting connection with individuals may not be an easy choice. However, the rewards of a loving, kind and genuine relationship make it one of the greatest choices you will ever make. We must invite the Lord in everything that concerns our lives, the Bible states, *"In all thy ways acknowledge him, and He shall direct thy paths,"* (Proverbs 3:6). Prayer can heal our relationships and give us direction when we feel at a loss about how to continue. It can help us understand a situation and keep us going when we do not feel like it. Through prayer, God will hold us close when we are hurting and provide guidance on how we can get over the challenges we are facing. Prayer can undo things inside of us, so we can move forward despite misunderstandings. When we pray, God works in our relationships in ways we cannot see.

Do not allow the winter season to sanction you to call it quits in a relationship that you hold dear. This could be with your spouse, children, friend, family member or co-worker. All relationships have their ups, downs, ebbs, flows and will go through winter seasons. Sometimes, the cause of the turbulence might be obvious and other times they are not but let what brought you together in the first place keep you together until you can get to spring again.

Everyone can enjoy and tolerate a relationship during the festivities of the summers and the fragrance of spring. At times, we fail to survive the cold and rigor of winter. If we learn to see our loved ones through the eyes of Christ, which is the eyes of love, we will be able to survive winter. If our relationships are worth anything, let's fight for it! Bundle up and face the cold with the hope that you will soon be able to enjoy spring gain.

Focus Scriptures

"Greater love hath no man than this that a man lay down his life for his friends." **(St. John 15:13).**

"A friend loveth at all times, and a brother is born for adversity." **(Proverbs 17:17).**

"He that covereth a transgression seeketh love; but he that repeateth a matter separateth very friends." **(Proverbs 17:9).**

"A man that hath friends must shew himself friendly: and there is a friend that sticketh closer than a brother." **(Proverbs 18:24).**

"Behold, how good and how pleasant it is for brethren to dwell together in unity!" **(Psalm 133:1).**

"A froward man soweth strife: and a whisperer separateth chief friends." **(Proverbs 16:28).**

"Beloved, let us love one another: for love is of God; and every one that loveth is born of God, and knoweth God." **(1 John 4:7).**

"To him that is afflicted pity should be shewed from his friend; but he forsaketh the fear of the Almighty." **(Job 6:14).**

"And this commandment have we from him, that he who loveth God love his brother also." **(1 John 4:21).**

"Iron sharpeneth iron; so a man sharpeneth the countenance of his friend." **(Proverbs 27:17).**

"And if one prevail against him, two shall withstand him; and a threefold cord is not quickly broken." **(Ecclesiastes 4:12).**

CHAPTER FIVE

Ministry / Spiritual Life

In my formative years I recall, religiously attending Sunday morning services with my mom. The service time was 8:00 am and to be quite honest I did not like attending but I had no choice. During the service I would find everything to distract myself so that the time could pass by quickly. Prayers were said from a book and the hymns they sang were boring in my estimation. As I got older, I realized that my family were members of the Anglican Church. I became a part of their girls' youth group called Daughters of the King, (DOK). My god mother was one of the leaders and so she signed me up without my consent. As time went on, I began enjoying the youth group. We would go on various outings such as beach trips, picnics and places of interest, things I would not be able to do because my mother simply could not afford them.

I continued to attend that church until my mother and sister stopped going. This worked for me because I no longer had to endure what I considered to be those boring services. My mom still encouraged us to pray, read our bibles and taught us good moral principles that she held us accountable for. The golden rule was, "do unto others as you would have them do unto you." Being successful in the country wide examination that placed students in High schools, I was privileged to attend an all-girls Catholic school. This meant that we had to participate in daily devotions and weekly masses. Holy Communion/ Eucharist (the eating of the Lord's body and the drinking of His blood), was also a part of the school's weekly agenda. I was not a Christian at that time or any religious guru, but I knew that one had to live a certain lifestyle to partake of this sacred sacrament. All my friends would participate because they saw it as something to do. I NEVER did because I knew that I was not worthy to do so.

A couple of years passed where I was not attending any church except for the mandatory masses and devotions at school. I felt fine with that as I considered myself a morally good young lady. Upon arrival home from school one day, I saw a group of individuals next door to my house. The house was for sale, so I thought they were prospective buyers who were looking around. Walking towards my door a man in the group called out, "hello" to me. He introduced himself as a pastor and told me his name. He stated that he was looking at the place for a church home for his saints. He asked me if I was saved. No one had ever asked me that question before, and honestly, I was not quite sure what that meant. So as not to appear unintelligent after all I was attending one of the more prestigious high schools at that time. My confident answer was, "Yes I am saved." Looking back at my answer I chuckled at the pride that exuded from me that day.

After our goodbyes I went in and told my siblings and mother that a church was coming next door to us. They were all amazed wondering what kind of church that was, I told them the pastor said they were Pentecostals. I was never exposed to that kind of doctrinal belief, this was new for me. They were not so thrilled about a church coming next to our home, everyone started talking about the negative impact it would cause namely noise and trafficking. About a month later, they were back cleaning and getting the place ready for their new church home. This was a regular house so what they did was erected a tent like structure with wooden planks supported by bricks for seating. The flooring was dirt, no concrete tiling or wood.

Curiosity is in my nature and so once they started having services I would go over and stand at the entrance and observed. I totally enjoyed the vibrancy and the energy that they put in their worship, a huge difference from what I was familiar with. They had services every night, and they called it revival. I would hurry home from school, got my homework and my chores completed so I could go over and listen to the service. My mom was not particularly keen about this because she had a problem with the loudness and the fact that they referred to everyone who were not saved as, "sinners." However, she never stopped me from going because she felt it was better than engaging in other activities that were unprofitable.

Each day I became more and more interested in what they were doing. I found myself now going in and sitting in the back rather than standing outside. I would stay until it was over and some night that could be 10:30 pm – 11:00 pm. I started making friends and they would share with me in depth what their doctrinal belief system entailed. They encouraged me to keep coming. At home I became their public defendant. Whenever my family members would say anything negative about them I would say that they were nice people. My consistent attendance and conversation with different ones brought me to the confession that I was a sinner and I needed to be saved. One night, for the first time after attending their services for six – months, I got the courage to walk to the altar. The emptiness and hunger that I felt for God was real. I cried out to Him putting all my pride and traditions aside. I just needed God.

One of the altar workers asked me if I wanted to be baptized, I answered, "yes", but then I remembered my mom who had consistently warned me not to be a part of that church. With that thought flooding my mind I quickly reneged on my yes. I did not want to be at odds with my mom. They told me to obtain permission from my mom because I was not considered a consenting adult at age seventeen. That night I went home feeling sad, I no longer wanted to be classified as a sinner. I needed to be saved and to become a part of the family of God. My mom was already in bed. I tried to enter the house without making too much noise, she heard me and reprimanded me for coming in late yet another night. Crawling into bed I prayed for the first time, not too sure if I was doing it right, I asked God to give me the courage to talk to my mom about getting baptized.

In the morning after a good night sleep I got up and went to school. Throughout the day my mind was preoccupied with being baptized and being saved. I could not wait for the school day to be over, I hurried home, did my homework, evening chores and waited for my mom to get home to ask the most dreaded question. The words could not sooner come out my mouth my mom said, "no". she also stated that if I did get baptized I could not come home. What was I going to do? I had nowhere to go and I wanted to be baptized. My begging and pleading did not change her answer, nevertheless I went over to the service as usual, it was such a blessing! Again, the altar call was given, I walked to the altar and requested baptism even though I knew what was awaiting me home. As the altar workers prayed with me before escorting me to change for baptism I prayed and ask God to let my mom be at peace with my decision. Fear and happiness collided but in that moment all I could envision was my new life in Christ. I was eagerly looking forward to it.

I remember my baptism like it was yesterday, back then we were not as sophisticated with baptismal robes and the frills that went along with it. I was given an old purple dress and a head wrap, the baptizer was dressed in old clothes also, neither of which mattered to me. Getting baptize was my primary focus and everything in that moment was nonexistent to me. He made me repeat my vow, not until friends forsake me; not until things get hard, not until my mother and father turn against me but it was until death. He quoted, *"And he said to them all, if any man will come after me, let him deny himself, and take up his cross daily, and follow me."* St. Luke 9:23. Upon the confession of my faith I was baptized on June 24, 1983 in the name of Jesus Christ for the remission of my sins. Oh happy day as floods of joy filled my soul. Those standing around began to sing, *"My young companion fare thee well I will not go with you to hell. I am on my way to Canaan's land I will not go I will not go with you."* Involuntary tears were streaming down my face I was finally immersed in water according to Acts 2:38, *"Then Peter said unto them, Repent, and be baptized every one of you in the name of Jesus Christ for the remission of sins, and ye shall receive the gift of the Holy Ghost."*

That night I delayed going home as long as I could. Everyone was so happy for me and promised that they would be there for me. Finally, it became apparent that everyone was just about gone so I fearfully went home. My mom was waiting for me by the door, she said, "Didn't I tell you not to go over there and wet up yourself?" She viewed my baptism as, "wet up", she harshly reprimanded me not to go over to the church ever again. In my mind I knew that could not be because I was now a part of the family of God and fellowship was a must. Before falling asleep I thanked God for giving me the courage to say yes to Him in water baptism and asked Him to work things out for me. I felt so blessed and full of excitement telling my close friends that I was now a Christian. Some were happy for me and others were indifferent. None of the reactions phased me, I was so happy to be a child of God. Like the Samaritan woman at the well who when she met Jesus left her water pot and ran in the city to tell others to come and meet Jesus. "*The woman then left her waterpot, and went her way into the city, and saith to the men, Come, see a man, which told me all things that ever I did: is not this the Christ?"* (St. John 4: 28 – 29).

The first couple of months in my Christian journey was a little rough, I was not able to attend all the services because of restrictions from my mom. I fasted and prayed about the situation and went whenever I could. The support structure from my church family was great. Whenever I was in attendance the saints lavished me with encouragement to hold on to Christ. However, not having the flexibility to attend services consistently broke my heart, but I was determined to stay the course. A couple years later in my Christian walk, my mother migrated to the United States to join one of my sisters. She was in search of a better life for her children. Her absence as head of our household gave me the latitude and freedom to immerse myself fully in my Christian walk. I would spend all my spare time with the saints, outside of service times I would go over and talk with those that lived on the premises. This was my new way of life, I considered it to be my new normal and I loved every moment of it. I was now free to go on church trips, attend every service and participate in all things church. I was now living my BEST life and the fellowship with the saints felt great.

I was filled with the Holy Ghost not many days hence. Having the Holy Ghost was an integral portion of our doctrinal belief. The infilling of the Holy Ghost was important because this denoted Christ in us. The Holy Ghost enables us to live for God and seals us until the day of redemption. *"And grieve not the Holy Spirit of God, whereby ye are sealed unto the day of redemption,"* (Ephesians 4:30). We also believed that, *"Neither is there salvation in any other: for there is none other name under heaven given among men, whereby we must be saved."* (Acts 4:12). Now that I was filled with the Holy Ghost, I got even more involved. I became a member of the choir, youth officer and Sunday school teacher. I enjoyed living and working for the Lord and the fellowship with the saints was priceless. The zeal I had for the things of God was unquenchable, like the Psalmist, *"As the hart panteth after the water brooks, so panteth my soul after thee, O God."* (Psalm 42:1). My daily desire was to get to know God in a deeper way. I wanted to know God like the Apostle Paul, in the power of His resurrection. *"That I may know him, and the power of his resurrection, and the fellowship of his sufferings, being made conformable unto his death;"* (Philippians 3:10).

Daily bible reading, weekly fasting, attending services, prayer and meditation served as catalyst to facilitate my spiritual growth. The desire to go on to perfection and not laying again the foundation of repentance was my goal. Spending time with the saints helped to quench my thirst for God. We would have informal bible discussions, and pray together, spurring each other unto good works. I became actively involved in going on the mission field where they were planting new churches. There was no formal means of transportation and we totally relied on God for favor to take us back and forth these out station churches. I was now in college and would get home in the wee hours of the morning with only a few hours sleep before going to classes. I recall once our transportation broke down and I got home the following morning. I only had enough time to shower, and head to class to sit a final exam. I had no time to look over my notes, but God rewards faithfulness and I was successful not only in that exam, but I was able to graduate from college with honors.

With the passing of time and years somewhere along the way I became distracted. I knew I still love God and wanted to continue to serve Him. Allowing the voices and actions of the naysayers and critics toward me to become my primary focus instead of God, I drifted in my commitment to all things God. My critics felt I was still too new to the assembly to be doing so much. Little did they know that God blesses whom He chooses, and that longevity is not God's prerequisite for service but instead a willing and obedient heart. I began listening to the wrong voices and started telling myself, "why bother?" Questioning my purpose and calling became the thing for me to do. The snow of winter had now blanketed my spiritual life, I had entered a season of dormancy and spiritual slumber.

My once blooming testimony and exhortation were now replaced with silence and complaints. Service attendance became sporadic as I kept myself busy with work, taking all the overtime that was offered. Prior to all the criticism directed at me I would not have done any overtime that affected my church commitment. I believed that the service of God was my priority and everyone at work understood that. My colleagues at work also noticed the change and questioned the change. My response was, "I needed the money." While this was not the whole truth, I had no intention of sharing with them my real reason for amassing all this overtime. The effectual fervent prayer life I had worked so hard to cultivate was replaced by lukewarm, drive by, unfocused prayers. Discouraged by the unexpected criticism and backbiting from within had me bent over and could not look up optimistically. After all I was doing the right thing, shouldn't I be praised for this? I was met with fierce opposition. Ideally, I should have run to God for help I allowed the cold, chilly winds and rain of winter to create freezing icicles in my spiritual life. My bible reading, and meditation became haphazard and my prayer journaling ended in a dull screech, I was struggling.

On several different occasions, some of the brethren offered me advice, shared their concerns and love for me. I refused to accept the warmth that they were attempting to provide me. I acted like everything was okay. I would justify my behavior with what I thought were reasonable excuses, which only prolonged the winter season. A feeling of apathy saturated me as I felt like everyone and everything was against me. The inconsistency in my daily devotion only plunged me into a downward spiral. Freezing from the feeling of isolation and self-pity I had allowed the negative comments and actions of others to affect my relationship with God. My spiritual energy was very low. The only lens I could see through was the one that read, "I don't deserve this treatment."

Proverbs 14:14 states, *"The backslider in heart shall be filled with his own ways: and a good man shall be satisfied from himself."* At this point that's how I felt, like a backslider. I was not stealing, killing or cheating but my dedication, fervency, and zeal was totally off. One Sunday morning I went to service and our pastor called for a twenty-one day fast. The first thing popped in my head was, I am not doing that. Immediately the war began in my members. The Holy Spirit was encouraging me to do it for my breakthrough, and the flesh was saying it will not make a difference. Like Paul I was wrestling, *"But I see another law in my members, warring against the law of my mind, and bringing me into captivity to the law of sin which is in my members."* (Romans 7:23). The state of luke-warmness penetrated every area of my spiritual commitment, I recognized that I desperately needed a change.

God's gentle nudges were unheeded as I continued in my spiritual self-destruct. He called but I could no longer hear His voice. His pressure ramps up, but my heart was numb. I was too upset and proud to ask for help. My spiritual growth had frozen, and only a miracle could thaw my spirit. I was iced in by a spiritual freeze-up and I didn't know what to do. Sounds like a bleak picture, doesn't it? However, the good news is, God still waits on the other side with warmth. sunlight, salt and whatever it takes to get us through the winter. That night, I decided that I would participate in the fast. I hurriedly said a prayer asking God to give me the strength I need to go through with it. Once upon a time that would have been my delight to draw closer to God and crucify the flesh and its desires. This time it seemed like a hike and an uphill climb.

To no surprise to me, the first few days fasting was rough, as I expected. Pushing against the sluggish and lethargic feeling that came upon me when it was time for prayer service, I still went. Seven days into the fast I felt like I was just going through the motions, and I wanted to quit. After service that night one of the mothers called me aside and encouraged me. She asked me if the Lord did me something wrong, that question took me by surprise and so it took me a while to respond. Finally, I said, "No," and she said, "Whatever you do don't let God down, continue to hold on to His hands." I felt her genuine care and concern as she held my hand and prayed with me. She hugged and assured me that everything would be alright. For the first time in months I felt a sense of belonging again and like someone truly cared.

The night following, I asked the same mother if I could speak with her. I confided in her about how I was feeling; withdrawn, disappointed and stuck. The moment I opened up a sense of peace enveloped me, I felt like a huge load was lifted off me. The healing process had begun, and everyday going forward I felt renewed strength. As I developed my relationship with God afresh, the joy of having a relationship with Him re-entered my life, filling me with fresh energy to continue with my walk with Him successfully. Daniel 2:21 states, *"And he changeth the times and the seasons: he removeth kings, and setteth up kings: he giveth wisdom unto the wise, and knowledge to them that know understanding."* My winter season was changing, and I was grateful! I could feel the temperature rising and the flowers beginning to bloom again. My relationship with God was getting stronger and I felt great.

Over the course of my Christian walk I have encountered many instances where I was talked about, criticized, accused wrongfully, cursed at, and slandered but that first experience taught me wisdom. The Bible offers encouragement with scriptures such as, *"But we have this treasure in earthen vessels, that the excellency of the power may be of God, and not of us. We are troubled on every side, yet not distressed; we are perplexed, but not in despair; Persecuted, but not forsaken; cast down, but not destroyed; always bearing about in the body the dying of the Lord Jesus, that the life also of Jesus might be made manifest in our body."* (2 Corinthians 4: 7-10). Now, I immerse myself in the word of God and align myself with likeminded individuals to ensure a support structure to hold me accountable. This helps me to maintain my focus and insulate me from discouragement.

Sometimes, our spiritual lives become dormant. There is no growth and we have lost our zeal and passion because we are not seeing the fulfillment of the promise of God in our lives and ministries. The dormant season is not a license to die in the process but instead let us use these moments as fertilizers to take us to our harvest. A diamond cannot be polished without friction, without the jeweler's chipping, grinding, polishing and buffing. Likewise, a life cannot be brought to its full potential without undergoing the hardship of winter. Very soon you will be enjoying a bountiful harvest!

Focus Scriptures

"When I was a child, I spake as a child, I understood as a child, I thought as a child: but when I became a man, I put away childish things." **(1 Corinthians 13:11).**

"Brethren, be not children in understanding: howbeit in malice be ye children, but in understanding be men." **(1 Corinthians 14:20).**

"That he would grant you, according to the riches of his glory, to be strengthened with might by his Spirit in the inner man;" **(Ephesians 3:16).**

"Till we all come in the unity of the faith, and of the knowledge of the Son of God, unto a perfect man, unto the measure of the stature of the fulness of Christ: That we henceforth be no more children, tossed to and fro, and carried about with every wind of doctrine, by the sleight of men, and cunning craftiness, whereby they lie in wait to deceive; But speaking the truth in love, may grow up into him in all things, which is the head, even Christ . . . But ye have not so learned Christ; If so be that ye have heard him, and have been taught by him, as the truth is in Jesus: That ye put off concerning the former conversation the old man, which is corrupt according to the deceitful lusts; And be renewed in the spirit of your mind; And that ye put on the new man, which after God is created in righteousness and true holiness." **(Ephesians 4:13-15, 20-24).**

"As ye have therefore received Christ Jesus the Lord, so walk ye in him: Rooted and built up in him, and stablished in the faith, as ye have been taught, abounding therein with thanksgiving." **(Colossians 2:6-7).**

"Lie not one to another, seeing that ye have put off the old man with his deeds; And have put on the new man, which is renewed in knowledge after the image of him that created him:" **(Colossians 3:9-10).**

"For when for the time ye ought to be teachers, ye have need that one teach you again which be the first principles of the oracles of God; and are become such as have need of milk, and not of strong meat. For everyone that useth milk is unskillful in the word of righteousness: for he is a babe. But strong meat belongeth to them that are of full age, even those who by reason of use have their senses exercised to discern both good and evil." **(Hebrews 5:12-14).**

"Therefore, leaving the principles of the doctrine of Christ, let us go on unto perfection; not laying again the foundation of repentance from dead works, and of faith toward God, Of the doctrine of baptisms, and of laying on of hands, and of resurrection of the dead, and of eternal judgment." **(Hebrews 6:1-2).**

"As newborn babes, desire the sincere milk of the word that ye may grow thereby:" **(1 Peter 2:2).**

"Ye therefore, beloved, seeing ye know these things before, beware lest ye also, being led away with the error of the wicked, fall from your own steadfastness. But grow in grace, and in the knowledge of our Lord and Saviour Jesus Christ. To him be glory both now and forever. Amen." **(2 Peter 3:17-18).**

CHAPTER SIX

Biblical Characters Who Endured Winter

Ecclesiastes 3:1, states, "*To everything there is a season, and a time to every purpose under the heaven.*" Solomon states that a time exists for everything. A time of dry season, much like the winter or that of a desert, during which you can mourn and weep, break down and keep silent. Please know that it is OKAY to have dry winter seasons in life, in fact it is 100% normal. When winter comes it leaves us searching for answers and a way out. There is a set time and duration for winter in the natural. However, in our lives sometimes this season takes us unaware and we are completely unprepared for it. Not knowing the duration of the cycle makes us even more concerned. Winter is a season existing to teach us how to completely depend on God. It also reveals our inability to live without Him. Every mile in winter feels like two. There is this urge to bypass the season if we could or cave in.

Winter is a season existing to teach us how to completely depend on God. It also reveals our inability to live without Him.

Everyone cycles through a series of seasons. If you try to stop the process and/or avoid a season, you will never be able to move past it and experience the others. Ecclesiastes 3:1, informs us that in our lives, there is an occasion for all things and a season for every activity. Whether you know it or not, the situation you find yourself in did not occur by happenstance. The hard, inescapable truth is that eventually we all go through the winter season; a time of nothingness, empty and void in between seed time and harvest. There may be a winter in our lives in which things that used to be fruitful for us die like leaves falling from a tree. Periods where beauty fades like that of roses, and our energy declines like a hibernating bear.

If you are going through a dry season where you feel lonely and isolated, or even just overwhelmingly fatigued, and tired of the challenges that life presents. Do not avoid it or try to deny its existence. Prepare yourself for the harsh times ahead and overcome the cold. Learn to endure the freezing temperatures. The rush of cold air on your cheeks. The crunch of snow beneath your feet and find warmth and comfort in the word of God. Winter does not last forever. Once it passes, spring brings a beauty and warmth to all things. It is exciting and a sigh of relief to know that spring is here. Whether you are a Christian reading this in search of spiritual guidance, someone who feels like you are stuck in a time, and nothing seems to bring joy or satisfaction. You can be assured that the winter season in your life will pass.

Winter looks different for all of us. No two of us have the same exact experience during our winter. Likewise, no two snowflakes look alike, however they render the same result. For some, it is considered a time where you can rest the soil, and feast on the

No matter where you find yourself during your winter season; figuratively grab your boots and hats, dress like an Eskimo if you must, and warm up with the blazing fire of the word of God and encouragement from others.

crops that you have reaped during the harvest. For others, it is a time to simply hang on, and to scuffle until spring gets here. Winter for some individuals is neither seed time or harvest, but for survival. No matter where you find yourself during your winter season; figuratively grab your boots and hats, dress like an Eskimo if you must, and warm up with the blazing fire of the word of God and encouragement from others. During these challenging seasons, the pressures of life can have you sledding down life's hill faster than the wind. You feel that you are about to explode like a bursting pipe from the freezing temperature of winter. Well, God wants you to know today that you can survive the winter! Winter did not come to destroy you. Look at yourself in the mirror and affirm the following, "I am not my winter." Do not allow your winter to define you, God's objective for your life did not change because you are experiencing winter. When they crucified the Savior and hung Him on the cross it was a moment of suffering and hardship for Him. The cross did not change His plans to redeem us from our sins. The Bible stated that, He endured because of the joy that was ahead, *"Looking unto Jesus the author and finisher of our faith; who for the joy that was set before him endured the cross, despising the shame, and is set down at the right hand of the throne of God,"* (Hebrew 12:2). Throughout the word of God, we have examples of individuals who survived their winter seasons. This offers us hope because the same God who brought them through is willing and capable to do the same for us.

HEALTH

While there are many characters that I could reference, my favorite is the woman with the issue of blood. *"And a woman having an issue of blood twelve years, which had spent all her living upon physicians, neither could be healed of any, came behind him, and touched the border of his garment: and immediately her issue of blood stanched. And Jesus said, who touched me? When all denied, Peter and they that were with him said, Master, the multitude throng thee and press thee, and sayest thou, who touched me? And*

Jesus said, somebody hath touched me: for I perceive that virtue is gone out of me. And when the woman saw that she was not hid, she came trembling, and falling down before him, she declared unto him before all the people for what cause she had touched him, and how she was healed immediately. And he said unto her, Daughter, be of good comfort: thy faith hath made thee whole; go in peace," (St. Luke 8: 43 – 48). Like this woman, you may be known by your winter. Isolated and rejected, spent all you have on doctors and medicine but still not well. However, she heard that Jesus was passing her way and as she waddled through the snow like a penguin. She mustered up the strength and courage to press through the crowd. Guided by the Holy Spirit, she moved quietly, inspirationally, passionately, and touched the hem of His garment. Immediately she was healed from her infirmities. Her actions speak of her belief. The woman moved beyond her own weak body to receive her deliverance. She was driven by the promise that He was the Great Physician. God in His grace and mercy empowered this woman and her weak body to leave her house and go out into the crowd to find Jesus.

What will you do in the winter of your health? Will you curse God and die? Will you give in to the report of the enemy? We must allow our faith to work for us. Keep in mind that we may not all be healed immediately like the woman in the text, but like Paul the Apostle it might be a situation where we are told to live with it. God told Paul that His grace was sufficient! *"And lest I should be exalted above measure through the abundance of the revelations, there was given to me a thorn in the flesh, the messenger of Satan to buffet me, lest I should be exalted above measure. For this thing I besought the Lord thrice, that it might depart from me. And he said unto me, my grace is sufficient for thee: for my strength is made perfect in weakness. Most gladly therefore will I rather glory in my infirmities, that the power of Christ may rest upon me,"* (2 Corinthians 12:7 – 9). However, God decides to bring us our deliverance we should be accepting because He knows what is best for us. Our sickness and ill health should not drive us away from Jesus but rather draw us closer. In moments of illness let us not charge God wrongfully but let us trust God for a favorable outcome, with Him it is a "win – win" situation. "*For we know that if our earthly house of this tabernacle were dissolved, we have a building of God, an house not made with hands, eternal in the heavens,*" (2 Corinthians 5:1).

FINANCE

Financial suffering is a reality in the lives of many Christians today. Many of us are familiar with the vulnerable moments of financial crisis when frost patterns on the windows of our finances are glaring. Questions such as; "Will I be able to get a job this month?" "Will I have enough money to pay rent?" "Will I be able to make my car payment?" "Will I be able to put food on the table for my wife and kids?" Seasons such as these represents the dark nights of winter. In 2 Kings 4:1 – 7, we read the account of the widow with the pot of oil. In the days of Elijah and Elisha in Israel, the principle prophets of God gathered a group of God's workers called "the sons of the prophets." These men worked tirelessly ministering to the prophets. One of these great servants died and left a wife and two sons.

The widow in our text was empty, broke and broken. She had no bread and no breadwinner. She had no employment or opportunity to be employed. Her two sons were not old enough to provide for her and now the creditor was at the door. Her creditor was calling for full payment of all that was owed. Out of her desperation she shared with Elisha her calamity. The cold of this winter must have sent shivers through her spine and she desperately needed a financial breakthrough. Her household was in debt and she had only a pot of oil. It was a season of bareness and despair for this widow.

In all this biting cold, the woman did not blame her deceased husband. Neither did she return to the weak and beggarly elements. She did not separate herself from the faith or abandon her family. Instead, she called out to God for help and was willing and obedient to hand over her little to receive God's abundance. The prophet did not ask the widow what she wanted he asked her what she had. In our financial struggle sometimes, we are looking for what we can get, and we withhold our giving, because we think we have nothing to give. God requested three things from the widow during her financial struggle and He is requesting the same of us. Bring what we have, bring what is available, and bring what is empty. Once she did that she had oil enough to sell, pay her creditor, and live from the surplus!

It may not always work out that you have surplus. In the case of the Apostle Paul, we can learn a rich lesson about enduring poverty and lack from Philippians 4:10–13, *"But I rejoiced in the Lord greatly, that now at the last your care of me hath flourished again; wherein ye were also careful, but ye lacked opportunity. Not that I speak in respect of want: for I have learned, in whatsoever state I am, therewith to be content. I know both how to be abased, and I know how to abound: everywhere and in all things I am instructed both to be full and to be hungry, both to abound and to suffer need."* This passage is well known for all the wrong reasons. Many well-intentioned Christians misuse, misinterpret, and misapply the divine promise of Philippians 4:13: *"I can do all things through Christ who strengthens me."* They assume that it means God will provide anything and everything they desire in this life. They cling to this verse like a lucky rabbit's foot, rubbing it while repeating the promise to receive all that they desire. For many, this includes monetary gain. This scripture unfortunately doesn't make that kind of promise. When read in context, we see that God promises contentment, not by pulling us out of financial suffering but by empowering us to endure it with contentment. We can do all things through Christ who strengthens us, and the world will notice it.

Paul penned these words from a prison cell. In the ancient world prisoners relied entirely on friends and family members to provide food and clothing unlike today. The state offered very little help. Paul was completely dependent on the mercy of others. He was vulnerable and in need. Suffering physically, and financially. Thankfully, the Philippian believers expressed their concern tangibly by sending material gifts to their imprisoned Apostle. Surprisingly, in response to the Philippians' generosity, Paul rejoices in the Lord, (Philippians 4:10). Their gift allowed Paul to experience relief from his financial suffering in prison. Paul declares, *"But I have all, and abound: I am full, having received of Epaphroditus the things which were sent from you, an odour of a sweet smell, a sacrifice acceptable, well pleasing to God,"* (Philippians 4:18). The Philippians' gift placed Paul in a state of material abundance.

And yet, Paul prohibits the Philippians from thinking that his joy in the Lord is entirely over their material gift. That is why he immediately includes a disclaimer, *"Not that I speak in respect of want: for I have learned, in whatsoever state I am, therewith to be content,"* (Philippians 4:11). Godliness with contentment is great gain, (1 Timothy 6:6), and even when we are experiencing financial hardships we are cautioned to be content.

CAREER

Career turbulence and job loss are times in our lives when it feels like freezing rain and dropping temperatures. Unfortunately, today individuals are considered successful by their career choices and job titles. Therefore, for some the loss of a job diminishes who they are. However, as believers our identity should be in Christ and we should see ourselves through the eyes of God. Our worldly positions and possessions or the lack thereof should not become the measuring stick of success for us. In St Luke 5:5, the disciples experienced a wintery night in their career as fishermen. They were expert at sea, and no doubt honed their craft but this night the scripture gave an account. They had toiled all night and caught NOTHING! *"And Simon answering said unto him, Master, we have toiled all the night, and have taken nothing: nevertheless, at thy word I will let down the net."*

Peter was very quick to object because they were professional fishermen and knew how to fish, and where to find the fish, and yet they fished all night long and caught nothing. The word "nothing" means "not even one" Their failure had nothing to do with how they were fishing or where they were fishing. Their failure came about because the Lord wanted to teach them a much needed lesson; that without Him, we can accomplish nothing! God will allow the enemy to rise-up on the job or cause you to be downsized just to show you where the fishes are. Probably, He wants you to go deeper but you are stuck in your own ideas. The minute the disciples obeyed Jesus's command they had the catch of their lives. They had to call others to assist. *"And when they had this done, they inclosed a great multitude of fishes: and their net brake. And they beckoned unto their partners, which were in the other ship, that they should come and help them. And they came, and filled both the ships, so that they began to sink,"* (*St* Luke 5: 6-7). Once they came to shore they forsook all to follow Jesus. God elevated them to a better position. They became fishers of men.

God will allow you to watch the snow fall on your career so that He can elevate you. Don't be distracted by the snowflakes or spindly branches laden with heavy snow. It is only a matter of time before you are promoted. Gideon was seen in the scripture doing an inferior job. He was found secretly threshing wheat in a winepress. It was probably because he had no other choice. The title given to Gideon, "mighty man of valor", didn't seem to line up with Gideon's current position. There he was, hiding in a winepress, trying to survive, and God was addressing him as a "mighty man of valor." In Judges chapter six, Gideon questioned, doubted, and inquired of God in fear. He could not wrap his mind around the fact that God, the Creator of the universe, was choosing and equipping him to do a mighty work for His people.

Remember that Christ calls us to, seek first the kingdom of God and His righteousness. *"But seek ye first the kingdom of God, and his righteousness; and all these things shall be added unto you,"* (St. Matthew 6:33). Being rooted in Christ is a fundamental "prerequisite" to finding God's will for your career. You will not be ready or able to find the career path He has designed you for unless you are seeking Him first. Place your life in God's hands and trust His guidance completely because He knows what is best for you.

RELATIONSHIPS

Human beings are social beings, and most of us yearn for close relationships with other people. Relationships require a lot of work and communication. Even with good open and honest communication sometimes we experience winter in some of our relationships. Sadly, the loving families, genuine friendships, and healthy relationships that we want most out of life often elude us. We need God to be the center of our lives for our relationships to thrive and grow past the winter seasons.

In Romans 12: 9 – 10, Paul gives the prescription for healthy relationships. If we consistently practice these qualities, our relationships will thrive. *"Let love be without dissimulation. Abhor that which is evil; cleave to that which is good. Be kindly affectioned one to another with brotherly love; in honour preferring one another;"* But maybe you are thinking, healthy relationships also depend on others. It's virtually impossible to have a good relationship with some people!" True. Paul acknowledged this when he wrote in Romans 12:18, *"If it be possible, as much as lieth in you, live peaceably with all men."* Sometimes, no matter what you do, some people are hard to get along with. But often if you treat a difficult person with the qualities that Paul enumerates in our text, they will change for the better in how they relate to you. But even if some relationships never improve, if you relate to others as Paul describes here, most of your relationships will be healthy.

An example of winter in relationship can be seen with Joseph and his brothers. They became jealous of him and decided to get rid of him. Joseph survived the pit and ended up in Potiphar's house over his affairs. After interpreting the dream for Pharaoh, he was promoted to governor over the affairs of the land and all the food that was grown in Egypt. The famine that Joseph predicted ultimately brings the sons of Jacob to Egypt.

With no other options, and hearing of excess grain in the neighboring country, Jacob's sons make a series of trips down to Egypt. Upon seeing his brothers some twenty years after selling him into slavery, Joseph conceals his identity and tests his family, locking up his brother Simeon until the rest of the brothers return with Benjamin. *"We be twelve brethren, sons of our father; one is not, and the youngest is this day with our father in the land of Canaan. And the man, the lord of the country, said unto us, Hereby shall I know that ye are true men; leave one of your brethren here with me, and take food for the famine of your households, and be gone: And bring your youngest brother unto me: then shall I know that ye are no spies, but that ye are true men: so will I deliver you your brother, and ye shall traffick in the land."* (Genesis 42: 32 – 34).

Choosing not to exact revenge, Joseph reconciles with his brothers and restores family unity by extending forgiveness, (Genesis. 45:1–15). Like Joseph, we should demonstrate forgiveness to heal and move on. Holding on to hurt and pain prolongs the winter and can result in the death of the relationship. The relationship that will overcome winter must consist of two forgiving individuals whose goals for the relationship are the same.

SPIRITUAL LIFE/MINISTRY

Unfortunately, all Christians have feelings of spiritual emptiness from time to time. Fortunately, God knew it would happen and has given us a lot of helpful advice in His Word. It doesn't matter how life makes us feel like God has forgotten us; the truth is, God cannot lie, and He said He would be with us to the end. It is often disobedience that causes our feelings of spiritual emptiness; or sluggishness in our daily devotion to Christ, that puts strain on our relationship with God. How we feel physically can impact how we feel spiritually. The best advice to overcome feelings of spiritual emptiness might be to first examine if we have been disobedient to God's commands for us. Ephesians 5:15–18 says, *"See then that ye walk circumspectly, not as fools, but as wise, Redeeming the time, because the days are evil. Wherefore be ye not unwise, but understanding what the will of the Lord is. And be not drunk with wine, wherein is excess; but be filled with the Spirit;"* We should also make sure we are doing all right physically. Are we getting enough sleep, eating properly, and exercising?" Taking care of ourselves physically is very essential to our spiritual health. If we are not well physically it hampers our worship, makes us feel sluggish and we don't have the strength to carry out spiritual responsibilities, like prayer, fasting and meditation.

David had a great relationship with God, He was considered a man after God's own heart. *"And when he had removed him, he raised up unto them David to be their king; to whom also he gave their testimony, and said, I have found David the son of Jesse, a man after mine own heart, which shall fulfil all my will,"* (Acts 13:22). God called, anointed and appointed Him to be King over Israel, but there was a time when winter existed in the relationship that David shared with God. His lust for women, and his idleness contributed to his adultery with Bathsheba. He violated not only her, but also her family, who had loyally served him. Rather than confessing his sin, David executed a murderous cover-up process, by placing Bathsheba's husband Uriah at the front of the battle. This resulted his death. This then led to more sins as David employed his cover up scheme which estranged him further from God.

David received freedom and mended his relationship with God when he accepted accountability for his actions and confessed His sins. Crushed with guilt and a downward spiral, he penned, *"Have mercy upon me, O God, according to thy lovingkindness: according unto the multitude of thy tender mercies blot out my transgressions. Wash me throughly from mine iniquity and cleanse me from my sin. For I acknowledge my transgressions: and my sin is ever before me. Against thee, thee only, have I sinned, and done this evil in thy sight: that thou mightest be justified when thou speakest, and be clear when thou judgest."* (Psalm 51:1 – 4). In grace, God forgave him, and their relationship was restored.

God desires us to be in right standing with Him. When Adam sinned, all of mankind's relationship with God was severed, but God made a wonderful promise of redemption back in the Garden of Eden. He promised that He would one day bring us back into good standing with Him. "And I will put enmity between thee and the woman, and between thy seed and her seed; it shall bruise thy head, and thou shalt bruise his heel," (Genesis 3:15). This promise was fulfilled when He sent His son Jesus Christ to die on the cross of Calvary. We must do whatever it takes to ensure that winter does not destroy our relationship with God. He did what He had to do to bring us justification, so we should do what it takes to maintain it. He died that we might have life and have it more abundantly. When the chilling cold of sin comes knocking at our heart's door, let us insulate ourselves so that we may be able to stand in the liberty where He had made us free. The spiritual season of winter is designed to produce the spiritual strength necessary for us to withstand storms and bear the weight of our ministry.

> ***The spiritual season of winter is designed to produce the spiritual strength necessary for us to withstand storms and bear the weight of our ministry.***

In the winter seasons of our lives, when the sun shines hot and the wind blows cold. We must find a way to embrace this unpredictable weather. Do not be deceived by the bright sunshine but rather bundle up to protect against the boisterous winds. In the winter, God pares away all that is unprofitable from our lives, so that we can have a bountiful harvest. When we accept the process of winter season, we will be better prepared for spring. Like the trees, we will be better for pruning; because we are stronger, more vigorous, and above all, more fruitful.

CHAPTER SEVEN

Winter Survival Tips

The battering gusts of winter are uncomfortable leaving our quivering bodies cold. We are not without hope because our hope is anchored in the promises of God. Here is some advice coupled with faith that we can practice, that we will be able to survive, and even thrive in our winter. Life is taking place internally, although it appears like everything dies. During winter, the focus of a tree turns inward. Fruit falls away. Leaves change color and drop. Yet while the tree appears barren and apparently lifeless on the outside, inside much is happening. The trunk of the tree grows another ring, building its core strength to endure the force of spring storms, stave off blight, and bear the weight of fruit in summer. At the same time, the tree stretches deep, extending and expanding its roots to absorb nutrients and develop a firmer base. In the formation of the soil, rings and roots develop through the practice of core disciplines like prayer, study, fellowship and service.

Here are some tips to survive winter. When the days are short, and the nights are long; when the accumulation of the snowflakes of life's challenges makes it nearly impossible to see the road ahead. Take courage knowing that the sun will come out tomorrow and melt away the snow bringing clarity to our lenses for the journey before us.

STAY WARM

Staying warm seems simple, and a no brainer but you do this by bundling up. Naturally one would not dress in shorts and tank top on a snowy winter day, but we would put layers on to keep warm. We would ensure that we are securely covered from the harsh elements of the season. Spiritually, the Bible tells us how to bundle up in Ephesians 6: 11 – 18, *"Put on the whole armour of God, that ye may be able to stand against the wiles of the devil. For we wrestle not against flesh and blood, but against principalities, against powers, against the rulers of the darkness of this world, against spiritual wickedness in high places. Wherefore take unto you the whole armour of God, that ye may be able to withstand in the evil day, and having done all, to stand. Stand therefore, having your loins girt about with truth, and having on the breastplate of righteousness; And your feet shod with the preparation of the gospel of peace; Above all, taking the shield of faith, wherewith ye shall be able to quench all the fiery darts of the wicked. And take the helmet of salvation, and the sword of the Spirit, which is the word of God: Praying always with all prayer and supplication in the Spirit, and watching thereunto with all perseverance and supplication for all saints;"*

All the different pieces of the armor serve as protection to keep us safe. Staying warm requires some work and effort on our part. It becomes our responsibility to put the armor on and we should not leave it up to chance. We should be deliberate, and intentional about doing so. For the natural winter season, we are very deliberate about how we dress to keep ourselves warm. We buy clothes that are even thermal in nature to ensure that we are protected. Some of us would spend hundreds of dollars on a certain brand of winter coat and cashmere sweaters because staying warm in the winter is that important to us.

Staying warm goes further than just the bundle up. We also ensure that we have a source of heat indoors. This heat may take the form of a furnace/fireplace, gas or electric heat. If you are like me during the winter months, you would love your house toasty and warm! I do not like to be indoors and having to wear layers of clothing. The usual temperature ranges between 75 – 77 degrees in my home, a temperature that makes me comfortable and enables me to perform at my highest capacity. When the temperature drops, and I am cold it becomes a huge distraction for me because I am unable to focus. I become miserable, frustrated and tired. Watching my oil needle at home has become my self-appointed role because I never want my oil to run out. To reheat a cold house and cold furniture takes a lot more time than to keep them warm in the first place. I take special care to order ahead of time to guard against that crisis. The same diligence should be applied to keep the spiritual temperature high and thus staying warm.

Cold can be a stealthy killer both in the natural and spiritual. It damages us before we realize it. The effects of frostbite are typically not felt when it's happening. It is only hours later we realize the seriousness of our injury. The key to surviving the spiritual winter climate we experience is warmth. We have got to stay warm because if we don't, it can result in injury or even death. We cannot afford to die in our winter season; heat is available from the Holy Spirit. You don't just wing it in the winter in our homes during-you must get dressed for the weather and keep your fire burning. This requires preparation and ongoing maintenance. Saturate yourself in the burning word of God. Layer yourself with individuals who bring warmth through their words of encouragement and hope. Ditch anything and anyone that causes your warmth to evaporate. In our homes during the winter, we insulate our windows and

Saturate yourself in the burning word of God. Layer yourself with individuals who bring warmth through their words of encouragement and hope. Ditch anything and anyone that causes your warmth to evaporate.

doors to block out unwanted cold air, which results in a drop in temperature. The same principle applies when you are going through your spiritual winter. Block out the naysayers and those that come to discourage and distract. Fan your secret furnace of prayer to ensure maximum heat. Snuggle up in your prayer closet. It will keep you warm and your Father which sees in secret will reward you openly.

You can still live a victorious life and be on fire for God even in your winter season. The devil does not control your thermostat-the gauge is in your hand and the Holy Spirit will provide the fire. Your pipes will not burst from being frozen if you stay warm! Get some hand and feet warmers by searching the scriptures, *"search the scriptures; for in them ye think ye have eternal life,"* (St John 5:39). Do not focus on the uncomfortable cold of winter, or the danger of ice-covered highways, let us think of the warmth that we can wrap ourselves in and be safe!

We need to make sure we don't allow our faith or our passion for God to grow cold. We need to keep the fire of God's love burning in our hearts by meditating daily on His word, like we keep a continual fire burning in our homes for warmth. We must strive to maintain a heart of thanksgiving and praise by spending time in His presence. This will keep the flames burning, and help the coals retain the heat.

FOCUS ON TODAY

Maintaining your focus during the winter season is crucial to one's survival, because it is easy to fall down the rabbit hole of distractions during this time. Our main focus, however, should be on the present–this day. I have struggled to live in the present during my winters. I was constantly troubled about tomorrow. A natural-born "thinker," I consistently prepare for the future or analyze the past. I have found from experience that this has consequences. When we are frequently distracted from the present moment, we become unhealthy, unhappy, unproductive, and unable to hear God. Being distracted during the winter months can result in slip and falls, which can lead to injury or even death.

Jesus cautioned His disciples, as He cautions us today about worrying over our physical necessities. Christ promise to meet our needs when we seek Him first. Therefore, we are not to focus on what we need in the future but concentrate on God's provision for us today. Even in your challenging seasons, God is STILL providing. He gives enough to keep us until our next harvest! *"And God is able to make all grace abound toward you; that ye, always having all sufficiency in all things, may abound to every good work,"* (2 Corinthians 9:8).

In addition, we know that God will work everything, pleasant or unpleasant, for our good because we love Him. *"And we know that all things work together for good to them that love God, to them who are the called according to his purpose,"* (Romans 8:28). Worrying will only make the winter season appears longer. When we focus on the things that are unpleasant, they become magnified. In the winter months we have the challenge of the days being shorter, and the nights are much longer. It is imperative that we maintain the right focus to prevent discouragement and distractions. We must keep a clear space between us and God because one cannot keep their eyes on what they cannot see. This goes for both physically or spiritually. Do not let the weather ruin your vision, or your productivity!

In Joshua 3:4, the children of Israel were commanded to keep 2,000 cubits distance between them and the ark of the covenant. That's about a half of a mile, and the purpose was so they would always be able to see the ark in all types of terrain. In our spiritual lives, when we fill the spaces with all kinds of conveniences and distractions about tomorrow, it becomes very difficult and even

> ***Do not become so pre-occupied with harvest time in your winter seasons, that you fail to enjoy the fluffy, white cotton snow bed that the season brings.***

impossible sometimes to see where the Lord is leading us. Do not become so pre-occupied with harvest time in your winter seasons. Then you will fail to enjoy the fluffy, white cotton snow bed that the season brings. The devil's intention is to have you distracted by tomorrow that you fail to see the blessings of today. We all have an obligation and a choice where we want to anchor our focus. We can choose to focus on tomorrow, our problems, our lack or on our purpose. When we focus on our purpose, the bitter frost of winter will not be able to steal our joy because we are knowledgeable that this too will pass.

In the winter of his prison, Apostle Paul encouraged the brethren in Philippi to, *"Rejoice in the Lord always: and again, I say, Rejoice,"* (Philippians 4:4). His cold, confining circumstance did not shift his focus. Paul boldly proclaimed, *"For to me to live is Christ and to die is gain,"* (Philippians 1:21). Do not be distracted by the bolstering winds, drop in temperature, freezing rain, and the plethora of conditions that accompany the season. Remember, keeping your eyes on the prize will serve as encouragement and fuel to keep you going. Do not use your energy to worry about tomorrow, use it to believe today!

EMBRACE THE SEASON

Lean in instead of resisting the season because it works better. Someone once said, "ride with the wave because it makes for a much smoother ride." We must learn to joyfully accept the season because in the absence of that we can become bitter and discouraged, thinking that the season of winter is working against us. Winter should not be feared. You should look at it as a part of the process to get to your destiny. You may be limping and bruised from the mishaps of winter, but you are growing stronger by the day. This can only be seen when you view the season through lens of appreciation. Winter helps to keep us in a posture of humility, so that we can better appreciate our harvest when it comes. James 1:2-4 supports this, *"My brethren, count it all joy when ye fall into divers' temptations; Knowing this, that the trying of your faith worketh patience. But let patience have her perfect work, that ye may be perfect and entire, wanting nothing."*

Depending on God's grace moment by moment is key to embracing the season. The Apostle Paul pleaded with God several times to remove the, "thorn in his flesh." Whatever the thorn represented, it was a difficult and painful trial, but God did not remove it. Instead, He offered Paul His grace, so that His power would be manifested through him. God will accomplish His good purpose for our lives regardless of the hindrances or weaknesses we experience. However, we must embrace that season of our life. Paul stated that, He would glory in his infirmities, that the Spirit of Christ may rest upon him. *"And lest I should be exalted above measure through the abundance of the revelations, there was given to me a thorn in the flesh, the messenger of Satan to buffet me, lest I should be exalted above measure. For this thing I besought the Lord thrice, that it might depart from me. And he said unto me, my grace is sufficient for thee: for my strength is made perfect in weakness. Most gladly therefore will I rather glory in my infirmities, that the power of Christ may rest upon me. Therefore, I take pleasure in infirmities, in reproaches, in necessities, in persecutions, in distresses for Christ's sake: for when I am weak, then am I strong,"* (2 Corinthians 12: 7 – 10).

Paul had to get to a place of acceptance, or he would have probably spent the rest of his days asking God to rid him of this thorn. Can you imagine? He would have missed out living his life to the fullest because he would have been so preoccupied with this messenger of Satan which came to torment him. At some point we must believe that God who brought us to this season of winter can keep us in the winter and bring us to our spring. Accept now that God knows what is best for you. Your next season of spring will be magnificent, and you will find yourself rested and planted just where God wants you to be. God has a process to bring us into our next good season, but we must trust that process so that we can see the fruits. Do not despise YOUR winter. Even though the temperature might be less than favorable, it is during these moments that God builds your tenacity and strengthens you for the task ahead.

Embrace every challenge and adversity that comes your way. Peter the Apostle encourages us to embrace our fiery trials, "Beloved, think it not strange concerning the fiery trial which is to try you, as though some strange thing happened unto you: But rejoice, inasmuch as ye are partakers of Christ's sufferings; that, when His glory shall be revealed, ye may be glad also with exceeding *joy,"* (1 Peter 4:12 – 13). No season is perfect. We must learn to adapt to the climate or moan, groan and complain in it. Make a determined decision to trust God and be content. Being content does not mean we never want to experience change. We all have things in our lives that aren't right, and areas we want to improve. But when we are content in Christ, we can have joy while God is working on those situations. Being resistant may cause us to miss what God is doing in that season of our lives. Remember, to everything there is a season, and our path to our destiny, is no less. See the season as a gift from God. Our fears will turn into trust and we will be able to survive. It's easy to feel your value when a season is fruitful, but in a barren desert-like season it is natural to feel useless. Your value is not only in what meets the eye, but it is in who God created you to be. The season of winter does not devalue you. Do not let it define you.

No season is perfect. We must learn to adapt to the climate or moan, groan and complain in it.

It is easy to praise God and embrace your season when you feel happy and there are plenty of positive things happening. Notwithstanding, when the testing times come we are ready to despise them, and charge God wrongfully. Keep in mind there are seasons of seedtime, waiting, and harvest. These are synonymous to seasons of testing and breakthrough. The difficult seasons are necessary for the good times to come. God wants us to stay connected to Him, because He is our power source. To unplug from

Him is detrimental in frigid weather. Imagine having a dead car battery on a lonely road in the dead of winter. The possibilities of what could happen if help is not received quickly could be devasting, and even lead to death. Remembering what is true will empower you to embrace your season.

Second hand spiritual knowledge will not sustain us during winter seasons. Simply being around spiritual people will not be enough. A prophetic word will not be enough. If you are okay with simply receiving a prophetic word from someone else in this hour, one will have a hard time during the winter seasons. This is a time to learn to recognize His voice for ourselves, and cultivate a deeper intimacy with God. We must become one with the plan and purpose of God for our lives that we do not miss a season of blessings. In embracing our winter season, we are affirming to God that He knows what is best for us, and that His desire for us is to prosper in the things that He has called us to. As difficult as it is embracing this bitter, cold and frigid season, there is a blessing in doing so. He promised that after you have suffered a while He will make us perfect. (1 Peter 5:10).

THRIVE

I know this step seems counter-intuitive. Nevertheless, horticulturalists will tell you that some crops can grow and are harvested in the winter. Some of the more popular ones are onions, potatoes, cabbage and peas. In fact, low temperatures provide the best atmosphere for them to grow. To thrive means to flourish or develop well. Rather than falling into despair and despondency, your winter season should be a time for you to flourish and become mature in areas of your life that you may have overlooked during the busyness of the summer and spring. The winter season is not just a season to survive or barely make it, but it is a time to grow and develop.

The tree for example is disrobed in winter, but it is not dead. It appears motionless to the visible eyes, but the roots are thriving and going down deeper, preparing for the next harvest. The tree prospers in winter, fulfilling its God-intended purpose. Although, to the unknowing eye, it sure looks barren. Without understanding of the season, we might only see the barrenness, and therefore equating a prospering life in God to the opulent tree in early spring, with leaves and fruit intertwined. We forget that this blooming comes forth because of the preparation that winter provides. If we do not allow ourselves to thrive and send our roots down deep during the winter season, we risk the blessing of an abundant harvest.

God's original plan for our life is that we grow and develop in Him, even in our winter. The season of winter if embrace allows our root system to grow. It is during this season that our roots can go deep in search of that Living Water. The Bible states, *"And the remnant that is escaped of the house of Judah shall again take root downward, and bear fruit upward:"* (Isaiah 37:31). Without a strong root system, we will not be able to be strong, grounded and settled. Every strong wind that blows our way will uproot us. It is in the darkness of our winter season that we thrive and develop. During this time, we are not merely surviving but we are growing deeper in God. Because our life is hid with Christ in God, we are expected to bloom, inspite of unfavorable conditions. No matter what our circumstances may be, when we are planted, and full of praise, the season we are experiencing should not stop our growth.

The children of Israel that were exiled in Babylon received word from Jeremiah that they were going to be in that situation for seventy years. Synonymous to a winter season they found themselves having to adopt to the climate of their environment. They had to learn a new culture, new skills, acquire the taste for new foods, and some may even have had to learn new trade. To survive their winter God admonished them through the prophet Jeremiah to thrive and be productive. In Jeremiah 29: 5-6, God advised them of ways that they could thrive regardless of the difficulties they were experiencing. *"Build ye houses, and dwell in them; and plant gardens, and eat the fruit of them; Take ye wives and beget sons and daughters; and take wives for your sons, and give your daughters to husbands, that they may bear sons and daughters; that ye may be increased there, and not diminished."* God wanted them to live their lives like they lived it when they were in Jerusalem, and not to lay down and die because they were outside their comfort zone.

Like the children of Israel, God wants us to live our lives to the fullest and without regrets. The season may be dark, harsh on our physical body, and at times take a toll on our emotions, but He wants us to thrive! He does not want us to diminish and die while we are having our winter moments, but instead He desires for us to multiply and be of good courage. Let us learn from these Israelites while they were in Babylon. Life is still worth living, even in Babylon! Babylon is NOT where the story ends. In Psalm 137, when they were asked to sing one of the songs of Zion. Their response was one filled with doom and lacked conviction of their knowledge of God. They answered that they could not sing the Lord's song in a strange land. "By the rivers of Babylon, there we sat down, yea, we wept, when we remembered Zion. We hanged our harps upon the willows in the midst thereof. For there they that carried us away captive required of us a song; *and they that wasted us required of us mirth, saying, Sing us one of the songs of Zion. How shall we sing the Lord's song in a strange land?"* Do not lose your song in the winter, an environment that you are not accustomed to. Remember God is with you wherever you are.

> ***Do not lose your song in the winter, an environment that you are not accustomed to, remember God is with you wherever you are.***

Thriving during difficult times must be an intentional act on your part. You must decide that you will grow and keep growing even though your conditions may appear less than favorable. Psalm 92:12 states, *"The righteous shall flourish like a palm tree, he shall grow like a cedar in Lebanon."* Because you are righteous no winter can kill or stop your growth. Use this season to your advantage! Create deeper views, stronger processes, and a time of preparation for what is to come. The promise of God is that; He will prepare a table for us in the presence of our enemies, so that we can feast instead of dying in situations and circumstances that were designed to kill us! Don't stop doing what God has called you to do and He WILL cause you to increase. Push through the cocoon of winter and experience the new growth of becoming a beautiful butterfly.

CONCLUSION

God orders and administrates life on this planet with a full and varied palette of times and seasons. The winter blizzards does something which the warm summer wind cannot. Each season is unique and brings with its essential factors to life and should not be despised. Paul the Apostle recognized this when he wrote, *"And we know that all things work together for good to them that love God, to them who are the called according to his purpose,"* (Romans 8:28). Everything may not look or feel good, but nevertheless it works together to make things better. Winter to some may not appear to have any good thing to offer. When it comes, individuals find themselves unprepared and frustrated by the dropping temperature. The depth of the snow and the bolstering winds become a distraction to the blessings that the season offer. The season of winter should not be feared. Those of us who know the Lord must understand, God has a purpose for His crops in the winter, He has an even greater purpose for us. Our winter was never meant to plentiful harvest He has in store for us.

Having experienced winter in different areas of my life, and the lasting lessons I have learned along the way, I have concluded that there is beauty and blessings in winter. It took me years if not decades to come to this life changing truth. Getting to the place where I can now embrace my winter seasons have been the game changer for me. I can now sit in that uncomfortable state because I know that it is not forever. The words of the Psalmist, *"Be still and know that I am God,"* (Psalm 46:10), has also helped me along the way, to trust God even when I am freezing from despair. This scripture reassures me that God is on my side and I can trust Him to do what is best for me. My experiences have taught me wisdom and patience. I no longer get upset, discouraged or fear that I will die from the cold when winter happens. I now view the season, as a stepping stone and a teaching moment. Winter helps me to see what my weaknesses, insecurities, fears and doubts are. It also creates a desperation, hunger and thirst after God, as I seek Him to lead and guide me through the treacherous snow of my circumstances.

My encouragement to you is to start regarding your winter as an uncomfortable advantage. Most of what God has for us is outside our comfort zone. Joseph was thrown in prison, Daniel placed in the lion's den, the Hebrew boys in the fiery furnace and Paul was beaten, shipwrecked and thrown into prison. After all that these men have been through, they all came out victorious and with a testimony of God's providential care. God has a way of growing us through painful predicaments for His grace and glory! Whenever you find yourself in a winter season see it as God's classroom with your one to one lesson. He is trying to give you an advantage, by teaching you something on a personal and intimate level. I believe;

If you find yourself in a financial classroom – God is trying to teach you stewardship!

If you find yourself in a relationship classroom – God is trying to teach you forgiveness and patience!

If you find yourself in a health classroom – God wants you to know that He is Jehovah Rapha your healer!

If you find yourself in a ministry classroom- God is trying to teach you how to walk worthy of the vocation for which you are called!

> ***Resist the reflex to come out of your winter prematurely. Stay in thriving mode and keep on living.***

If you find yourself in a career classroom – God is trying to teach you that your steps are ordered by Him!

Be grateful that God has chosen you to be intimate with. The lessons that you will be privileged to learn in the classroom of your winters, will help you to overcome future trials. The Psalmist David learned many life changing lessons, and shared with us in Psalm 20:1, that the Lord WILL hear us in the day of trouble, and that He will defend us. With that knowledge, he was able to go through numerous winter seasons with a positive attitude of prayer. James 1: 2-4 encourages us, *"my brethren, count it all joy when ye fall into divers' temptations; Knowing this, that the trying of your faith worketh patience. But let patience have her perfect work, that ye may be perfect and entire, wanting nothing."* It is during the dry and desolate season of winter that we must be patient and trust God to bring us through. He wants us to stand still and see His salvation. Resist the reflex to come out of your winter prematurely. Stay in thriving mode and keep on living. Do not fear the elements around you that cause pain and uncomfortable moments. God is doing a work to perfect us. So patiently endure you will receive His promises.

Every day of our winter season will not be filled with, "hallelujahs" and "thank you Jesus". No association that you align yourself with can prevent you from experiencing winter. Your affluence, degrees and title cannot shield you from the bone chilling temperature of winter. Stop looking at your neighbor's summer and spring with envy. The truth of the matter is, they had to endure their winters to get to the harvest you see them reaping. Your level of anointing does not prevent you from facing winter. Remember, Job was perfect, upright, feared God and eschewed evil (Job 1:1), but that did not exclude him from the winter blues. Like Job, our winter is going to fall on a day, that we have NO control over. The Bible states, *"now there was a day when the sons of God came to present themselves before the Lord, and Satan came also among them."* Although Job did not understand why he was going through this harsh season, in all this he sinned not, neither did he charged God wrongfully! Job demonstrated trust in God even when everything around him was falling apart.

Your winter may not change with one prayer and one praise but find a way to give God thanks. During your winter season giving thanks can be hard to do. Everything around us may not look and feel like there is anything to give Him thanks for. Some winter mornings when you wake up, "thank you Jesus," may not be the first thing on your mind. You may feel let down because this is not how you envisioned your life. You may have thought that you would be enjoying the rich harvest of your labors, and the sunshine of our dreams, but winter came. Take the time to evaluate your winter season, be real and authentic about your feelings. Do not hang your harps on the willows forever. Our winter season can silence our praise and challenge our thanksgiving but be determined and praise Him inspite of!

The children of Israel failed to realize that singing the Lord's song was not subjected to a place but rather about the presence of God. According to Psalm 137: 1, they wept when they remembered Zion. For them, Zion signified the place where God is. Guard yourself from associating the presence of God in your life, only when you are basking in the spring, summer and fall season. This is a deceptive lie that the enemy would want us to believe. God is always present with us no matter what season we are encountering. He is a God that tabernacles with His people. There is nowhere we can find ourselves that God is not present.

Anyone can shout and trust God when they have good health; when the bills are being paid and there is reserve in the bank account; when all the relationships are going great and you can feel loved; when you are being promoted or have the job you dreamed of; your ministry is doing well and you see your name in lights. With that God is not impressed. God is impressed when you are facing winter challenges that could take you out, but you still find a way to give Him praise and trust in His able power. The power of remembering should be harness in our winter seasons. This helps to strengthen our resolve as a child of God. When we remember what God has brought us through, and His mercy towards us, we have a reason to endure our winters. Weeping may endure for a night, but joy is coming in the morning. (Psalm 30:5). Winter is ONLY for a set period. It does not last always. It has a beginning and an end, so you are well able to overcome it!

I admonish you to trust the process God has for your life. Your winters are an integral part. To trust the process means, to have faith in the divine plan that God has for your life. Even if that plan is hard and painful. Cultivate an unbreakable sense of trust if you do not understand the events that are unfolding and unravelling all around you. Tell yourself that the reason you are facing this winter season is because God is rearranging and arranging circumstances for your good. When the noise and the chatter of winter blocks your route to God's ears, leaving you stranded, and lonely on a cold winter night, you MUST continue to trust God! Paul stated, *"Being confident of this very thing, that he which hath begun a good work in you will perform it until the day of Jesus Christ,"* (Philippians 1:6). God WILL complete that which He started. The seasons of your life DOES NOT conclude with winter! Paul said, *"Thanks be to God, which giveth us the victory through our Lord Jesus Christ,"* (1 Corinthians 15:57).

When the noise and the chatter of winter blocks your route to God's ears, leaving you stranded, and lonely on a cold winter night, you MUST continue to trust God!

You may be faced with challenges ranging from;

- Sickness in your body
- The loss of a loved one
- The loss of a job
- Your home is in foreclosure

- You were next in line for a promotion, but was skipped over
- Waiting on the ideal spouse, and the nights are long and lonely
- Trapped in an abusive relationship
- Toiling all night but like the disciples you have caught nothing.

By no means is this an exhaustive list. It is in these moments of uncertainty that God shows us that He is in control. God wants us to trust our unknown future to a God who holds and KNOWS the future. He has an expected end for all of us, and a purpose for our winters. The God that we serve is not unrighteous, He has a reason for our struggles and a gift for our faithfulness! We must be persistent, focus, and determine as we forge ahead during our winter season. With faith in God and a prayer you WILL get through the season. The winter you are faced with is no match for the God that dwells on the inside. No matter how cold it gets, how lonely it becomes; how treacherous and slippery the road gets, remember that God is faithful, and we MUST trust His faithfulness. God is the God of divine happenings, *"Wait on the Lord: be of good courage, and he shall strengthen thine heart: wait, I say, on the Lord,"* (Psalm 27:1). Job knew something about waiting on God in his winter season. He said, all the days of his appointed time he would wait until his change come. (job 14:14). Job's change came after a long winter of silence and criticism as he sought answers from God. Little did Job knew that the teacher is always silent during a test. Do not allow the silence to deter you from going through your winter.

The winter you are faced with is no match for the God that dwells on the inside.

God will be with you as you face your challenges:

- If He can shut the mouth of the lion for Daniel
- If He can part the Red Sea for Moses

- If He can make the sun stand still for Joshua
- If He can open the prison door for Peter
- If He can put a baby in the arms of Hannah and Sarah
- If He can raise Lazarus from the dead
- If He can make blind eyes to see
- If He can make deaf ears to hear then surely, He can see you through the toughest of winter.

Paul also encourages us, *"And be NOT weary in well doing for in DUE season you shall reap if you FAINT not!"* (Galatians 6:9)

God's presence is ALWAYS constant, and His TIMING is ALWAYS perfect. He did not expose you to your winter to leave you. Take courage, consistently pray and passionately praise. Your winter season WILL come to an end. Beloved, God's plan for our lives far exceed what we can see with our own eyes. It is bigger than ANY winter we could ever face!

God's presence is ALWAYS constant, and His TIMING is ALWAYS perfect.

Be Bless!

ABOUT THE AUTHOR

Dr. Sandra Bailey is a strategic thinker and a lover of life. She is a multi – talented international Evangelist, public speaker, thought leader, life coach, radio show host and the author of *"Called to Worship - A Lifestyle of Praise"* and *"Overcoming Job Loss-A Spiritual Guide"* and co-author of *"Water's Edge Volumes I & 2– A 31 Day Devotional."* Born in Jamaica, West Indies, Sandra migrated to the USA to join her mother and siblings. She resides in Englewood, New Jersey with her loving husband Ian of 28 years and her daughter Sanian.

Sandra serves as a minister at the Church of Jesus Christ (Apostolic) in Englewood, NJ. She possesses a strong educational background which has culminated with a Doctorate in Theology, a Master's in Theology and a Bachelor of Science in Nutrition and Dietetics. Sandra believes that the combination of her victories, and challenges have made her into the respected mentor she has been. Additionally, Sandra is the co-owner along with Dr. Sharon Maylor of *Water's Edge Network, LLC.*, a life empowerment and strategic consulting company, and the co-visionary of the conference, "From Average to Awesome – Living A Life of Excellence." This conference is held annually in October.

Giving back is at the core of her being, and so she serves as secretary for the Mind, Body and Soul Health Ministry, New Jersey chapter. This is a charitable organization that gives back to the underserved of Jamaica and other Caribbean countries. She is also the Vice President for the Bergen county chapter of the Jamaica Organization of New Jersey, (JON – J).

When she is not wearing all these hats, Sandra likes spending time reading, relaxing with friends or at the spa.

Dr. Bailey believes in moving forward and lifting. She blazes the trail in mentoring and assisting individuals to maximize their potential. Her mantra is, "Nothing is impossible with God." She can be contacted at **sandrab.bailey@gmail.com**.

Printed in the United States
By Bookmasters